How to Survive Getting Into College

Rachel Korn, Special Editor

Hundreds of Heads Books, LLC
Atlanta, Georgia

Cover photograph by PictureQuest
Cover and book design by Elizabeth Johnsboen

Library of Congress Cataloging-in-Publication Data

How to survive getting into college / Rachel Korn, special editor.
p. cm.
ISBN-13: 978-1-933512-05-1
ISBN-10: 1-933512-05-9
1. Universities and colleges—United States—Admission. 2. College choice—United States.
3. College student orientation—United States. I. Korn, Rachel.
LB2351.2.H6784 2006
378.1'61'0973—dc22

2006019553

See page 257 for credits and permissions.

HUNDREDS OF HEADS BOOKS, LLC
#230
2221 Peachtree Road, Suite D
Atlanta, Georgia 30309

ISBN-10: 1-935512-05-9
ISBN-13: 978-1-933512-05-1

Printed in U.S.A.
10 9 8 7 6 5 4 3 2 1

How to Survive Getting Into College

WARNING:

This guide contains differing opinions. Hundreds of heads will not always agree. Advice taken in combination may cause unwanted side effects. Use your head when selecting advice.

CONTENTS

THE HEADS EXPLAINED

With hundreds of tips, stories, and pieces of advice in this book, how can you quickly find those golden nuggets of wisdom? We recommend reading the entire book, of course, but you can also look for these special symbols:

Remember this significant story or bit of advice.

This may be something to explore in more detail.

Watch out! Be careful! (Can we make it any clearer?)

We are astounded, thrilled, or delighted by this one.

Here's something to think about.

—*The Editors*
and Hundreds of Heads Books

Introduction

College might be called the best four years of your life, but you have to get there first. With selectivity rising, SAT and ACT tests to study for and take, applications and essays to complete, school visits and presentations to manage, grades and activities to maintain—and then the nerve-wracking wait for colleges and universities to select *you*—getting into college has become, truly, a grinding "process" in recent years.

As a former admissions officer and current private college counselor, I know how complicated it can seem, and how hard it can be to sort out all the options, advice, and suggestions. Somewhere in the middle of it all, we hope, there's the school of your dreams, looking for the student of its dreams—you! A perfect match.

Applying to college is a stressful period for families. It has spawned several cottage industries, such as test preparation and private counseling, and plenty of books and Web sites purporting to tell all and give you secrets and keys to admission (hey, you are reading this book, aren't you?). In some communities, college prep begins well before high school! Parents are more involved in the process than ever before: in some cases, their involvement has turned to over-involvement, and their children's colleges have also become their personal status symbols. Parents have been heard to speak of "our" application, instead of about "my child's" application. These changes have increased the race for the "edge" in the application that will yield that letter of admission. Families believe they have to play games of strategy to gain admission into "brand-name" schools—nothing less will do—and, along the way, the ideals of higher education may get lost.

But here's the truth: Admissions officers are bound by their instructions about whom to admit, and there is no way to *really* have an edge. An accomplished student who is merely building his résumé is as obvious to an admissions officer as the truly curious and passionate student who does things for love.

So how do you interpret and survive this rat race? Trust that there is some logic and sanity to it all, and that admissions officers invest themselves personally in their applicants. Assess your realistic chances of admission by genuinely evaluating your grades and skills against the colleges' averages. Craft thoughtful and reasoned applications to each school, and only apply to schools that you can truly imagine attending. Know that admissions are never guaranteed. Know that you are not defined by your rejection from—or even your admission to—a particular school. Great students can receive rejection letters simply because there's no room, and it is no reflection on their skills or character.

There are plenty of guides to help you get to college. What makes this one different? We don't rely solely on the advice of one or two experts: We've also consulted hundreds of people who have "been there, done that," and have a story to tell and advice to share.

In *How to Survive Getting Into College*, the 12th book in the Hundreds of Heads® series, we asked a variety of students, from Ivy Leaguers to small-college scholars to students at Big Ten universities, about their admissions experiences. We've also complemented our stories with hard facts and clear guidance on issues such as essay writing, interviewing, getting recommendations, dealing with financial aid, and taking the SAT. You'll hear what admissions officers, or AOs, are really thinking about on the other side of the desk, and the resident expert (that would be me) will answer some questions you've been afraid to ask: Trust me, AOs know and understand the secret thoughts, schemes, and fears of high school students.

We've talked to parents of students as well—after all, more and more parents provide support to their kids in the college search, whether as research assistants, travel agents, proofreaders, or bankers. And although this book is primarily for students, we all know who else will be reading it. (Note to students: Parental comments are headlined as such, or marked with a P, to make it easy for you to continue to avoid any more parental advice. But you should take a look; they have some pretty smart things to say.)

Think of this book as a companion guide to your college admission process, one that will help you reach the goal of this long journey: To find a place where you can be yourself, grow up, and enjoy the best four years of your life. Here's to the first steps on the path.

RACHEL KORN

First Steps: Launching The College Process

Your guidance counselor wants to see you. You receive brochures in the mail from places you've never heard of. Yes, it's time to start thinking about college. And while you have a lot of dreamy ideas about colleges, you also have a lot of competition for the top spots. Your graduating class is likely to be among the largest—if not the largest—in U.S. history. So: When, where, and how do you start? Read on to hear about other students' first steps toward college.

IT IS NEVER TOO SOON TO START preparing for college. You really have to assess your interests and skills well before you are accepted to a college and choose a major. Then you can properly choose the right career path for yourself and take relevant steps that will serve as a solid foundation for the first steps of your career. For instance, if you know you are good at writing, work at a newspaper during high school. Experience is key in any field.

—*Carly Jacobs*
Philadelphia, Pennsylvania
La Salle University

YOU DON'T HAVE TO IDENTIFY YOUR NUMBER ONE CHOICE AT THIS POINT.

—*Steve Detetriadis*
Parkersburg, West Virginia
West Virginia University

- It's never too soon to start preparing for college.
- Take advantage of information sessions when college representatives visit your school.
- Start refining your search in general first: Big campus vs. small; public vs. private.
- Organization is essential to keep information and deadlines from slipping through the cracks.
- If you know what you want, early decision can spare you a lot of stress.

FIRST, CONSIDER the important things: big city, college town, or something in between? Big school, small school? Liberal arts or specialist? Close to home or far away? Do they have the major you are considering?

—*Sarah Bormel*
Baltimore, Maryland
Boston University

I STARTED LOOKING FOR COLLEGES when my daughter was in middle school and began taking her, at any opportunity I could, to see the campuses. I wanted to be sure we had enough time to be involved in this without being stressed.

—*Anonymous*
Philadelphia, Pennsylvania
P Sarah Lawrence College

APPLYING TO COLLEGE IS HARD. The organization that is required to get all these things out and the time and the effort you put into the essays is phenomenal. And the terror that you feel: Is it worth all of this? Am I going to get in? Or am I going to get the thin envelope? You just have to remember: It will be over someday. You'll get in somewhere. It will work out.

—*CHRISTIANA*
NEW YORK, NEW YORK
COLUMBIA UNIVERSITY

KNOW YOURSELF. I've proven that I have some difficulty making big decisions and feeling confident in my choices. Early decision was definitely the best way to go for me. If you have an idea where you want to be, single out one school where the location, academics, atmosphere, etc., would please you. If you're leaning towards one school, apply early. This way if you get in, the decision is made. If you don't get in, you still have the opportunity to get into other schools through regular decision.

—*KATIE*
NEW YORK, NEW YORK
NEW YORK UNIVERSITY

TO GET YOUR CHILD TO APPLY to a broad range of schools, make it a condition of writing the checks for the application fees. First, point out that although the student is wonderful, the competition is fierce, as are the demographics. The reality is you have to try to increase your chances by applying to a range rather than within a narrow band, be it region, academics, status, or something else.

—*ANONYMOUS*
BROOKLYN, NEW YORK
P STATE UNIVERSITY OF NEW YORK,
PURCHASE COLLEGE

IF YOU NEED A GOOD REASON

A four-year college graduate earns 70 percent more than a high school graduate does.

PARENT TO PARENT

MY SON DIDN'T START THE COLLEGE APPLICATION process until he was a senior, and for him that worked. I think it's different with each kid. Some are ready to get down to brass tacks in eighth grade. Jeremy was not. We would have been knocking our heads against a wall if we tried to get him to think about college four years ago. But this year he was ready.

—JIM INGE
MORGANTOWN, WEST VIRGINIA
P

• • • • • • • • •

I TOLD MY DAUGHTER IN 9TH GRADE to start thinking about what she wanted out of life and to figure out how she was going to get there. That's the thing kids don't get: Until you set the goal, you can't determine the right path. She blew off most of the college prep stuff until she was a junior. I would have liked her to start earlier, but it worked out OK.

—TRINA AMAKER
NIKEP, MARYLAND
P UNIVERSITY OF MARYLAND

• • • • • • • • •

LISTEN TO WHAT YOUR KIDS WANT in their college experience. They know better than you do. My daughter was a top tennis player, so we applied to school with that in mind. Advice to parents: Don't stress too much! I really don't believe in a brand-name college education, but we get in the trap of wanting that for our kids. That won't necessarily be best for them. My son is 15 now, and I've told him that for the next two years he needs to do something he really, really loves so he can discover what he'll look for once college arrives.

—S.R.
SARASOTA, FLORIDA
P VANDERBILT UNIVERSITY

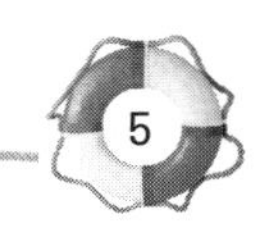

CREATE AN E-MAIL ACCOUNT that you will use exclusively for college admissions information, and make sure you check it often. There are so many free e-mail sites, you have plenty to choose from. More colleges are connecting with students through the Internet now. Some schools even notify you of your admission decision via e-mail instead of by letter.

—*LINDA ROADARMEL*
PARKERSBURG, WEST VIRGINIA
WEST VIRGINIA UNIVERSITY

WE STARTED TO TALK about specific colleges the summer after my daughter's sophomore year. Our first campus visit was that summer. By January of junior year, our mailbox was overflowing daily with letters and college catalogs.

—*DEBBIE*
PITTSBURGH, PENNSYLVANIA
P OHIO UNIVERSITY

If you know what you want to study, see who recruits for that field on the campus and make the connection before you apply to the school.

—*AMANDA NELSON*
NEW YORK, NEW YORK
UNIVERSITY OF WISCONSIN

I BEGAN THINKING about and searching for colleges around the start of senior year. This put me at a disadvantage because other kids I knew had been planning for college, in one way or another, since 9th grade. While I was playing on sports teams, other kids were planning out every extracurricular activity based on whether it would help them get into a better college. Although these kids probably had an advantage over me in searching for colleges, I think that I had a more exciting and enjoyable high school experience.

—*NATHANIEL COHEN*
WEST HARTFORD, CONNECTICUT
NEW YORK UNIVERSITY

FIRST, FIGURE OUT WHAT you want to study. The degree I wanted—marine biology—wasn't a popular one. And I'm from Chicago, so there were limited options around there. The degree automatically ruled out a lot of schools, which was a bummer. But I researched and eventually found a few places for me.

—*Dustin Johnson*
St. Petersburg, Florida
Eckerd College

WE STARTED THINKING about colleges the summer before David's junior year of high school. The process began by looking at types of schools, not specific schools. For example, we went to a big-city school, a campus school in a small town, and a campus school in a big city. It was good to see many different campuses.

—*J.K.D.*
Pittsburgh, Pennsylvania
P Kent State University

You can't prep for college too soon. I have injected myself with the SAT guides so that my unborn children can get an earlier start than I got!

—*Daniel*
Toronto, Ontario
York University

DON'T APPLY SOMEWHERE just because it has a name. It is no good being unhappy in a school that is too demanding or too far from familiar surroundings, or where the culture is alien. Try to be happy.

—*Anonymous*
New York, New York
P Carleton College

IT'S NEVER TOO EARLY TO START THINKING about college, and once you get into high school, you really need to think about making good grades from your freshman year on.

—*Ashley Yow*
San Antonio, Texas
Texas State University

HANDS-OFF PARENTING

REMEMBER, IT'S YOUR KID WHO IS GOING TO SCHOOL, and not you. As a parent you tend to think in terms of what you would want for yourself. But you have to adjust that thinking for what is best for your child. It's a different kind of thinking, but it is really important. For instance, if I was the one going to school, being away from home would be important. But for my son, he needs to have the support of his friends. He'd struggle away from here. You have to keep that sort of thing in mind.

—*JIM INGE*
MORGANTOWN, WEST VIRGINIA
P

I ALLOWED MY DAUGHTER TO GO THROUGH THE PROCESS on her own. If she is old enough to attend college, she should be independent enough to write her college essays and fill out the applications. However, stay involved with your children's progress. Discuss their goals with them. And help them be realistic about where they are applying.

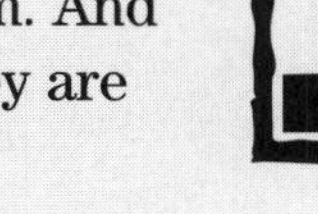

—*ANONYMOUS*
P

THE APPLICATION PROCESS can be a bit stressful, so it was nice to knock all of it out early and enjoy my senior year. In my case I was recruited late in the spring semester of my junior year and had to apply in April. Even though I don't recommend this, it can be done. I had all the information and test results accessible already. I had an awesome senior year.

—JOSIAH WHITE
CARROLLTON, TEXAS
OKLAHOMA BAPTIST UNIVERSITY

THE MOST IMPORTANT STEP early in the process is identifying what part of the country you are planning to go to school. I was applying to schools all over the country, basically based on the college football teams that I liked. I thought it would be cool to be accepted by Michigan and USC, but in the back of my mind I knew I'd never be able to afford to live in those areas. So all I really did was waste time.

—STEVE DETETRIADIS
PARKERSBURG, WEST VIRGINIA
WEST VIRGINIA UNIVERSITY

ASK THE EXPERT

What is an AO? Do AOs have special training?

An admissions officer, or AO, is responsible for visiting high schools, making presentations, reading and evaluating applications, and managing a section of the admissions office's internal responsibilities. An AO is rigorously trained in evaluating applications for his school, and this also includes training about understanding applicants' environments.

HEADS UP: IMPORTANT STEPS IN RESEARCHING COLLEGES

- Define your needs. Ask yourself the following questions to start assembling a preliminary list: What do I want to study? Am I seeking a broad-based liberal arts school or a school with a professional major? Do I want a public or a private school? What size do I want? Do I want to be close to home? Do I want to be in a city, town, suburb, or rural location? What atmosphere do I want: conservative or liberal? Serious or fun? Do I want a single-sex college or one with a religious affiliation?

- Use the Internet. You will find several Web sites that can help you compare and contrast schools and give you some basic information.

- Contact colleges directly through their Web sites and put yourself on their mailing lists. In addition to information, you will automatically receive their applications in the mail the summer before your senior year.

- When taking the PSAT or the PACT, fill in the bubble allowing schools to contact you. You will be contacted by colleges that believe your scores and profile indicate that you could potentially be a successful and /or interesting applicant.

- Ask questions of older high school students about the application process. Peers who have been through it may have words of wisdom. However, beware: There are thousands of colleges and universities across the country; your match may not be the same as your friends' matches, so investigate the schools that are right for you.

WHY GO TO COLLEGE?

You are not the first to wonder if college is for you. And with everyone and his mother (not to mention your own mother) telling you that you need to go to college, there naturally comes the voice of the devil's advocate who wants you to consider other options—like going to Europe, or Colorado, or a desert island, and just "being." So, why go to college?

AT FIRST, I WASN'T GOING TO GO TO SCHOOL. But then I realized it could change my life for the better.

—JODI
PITTSBURGH, PENNSYLVANIA
SETON HILL UNIVERSITY

• • • • • • • •

IN TODAY'S WORLD IT'S VIRTUALLY IMPOSSIBLE to get a really good job without college. There are just too many grads out there looking for work to think that you are going to walk into some HR office and have them hire you. I want to be an engineer, and I have a good aptitude for science and math, but without a college background and a college degree, nobody in the world is going to hire me. There are no *Good Will Hunting* situations going on out there in the real world.

—BILL LAWRYK
FREDERICK, MARYLAND
GEORGE WASHINGTON UNIVERSITY

• • • • • • • •

YOU GO TO COLLEGE TO BETTER YOURSELF. You don't want to be a loser your whole life.

—KIRA
ST. PETERSBURG, FLORIDA
SPC/PTA PROGRAM

WHY NOT GO TO COLLEGE? Why not live on your own, gain independence, meet new people, and get a degree that will get you a rewarding job doing what you love?

—*MAREN REISCH*
GENEVA, NEW YORK
KNOX COLLEGE

I WANTED TO GO TO COLLEGE SO THAT I could achieve the highest level of education possible, and so I could provide for and be in control of my future and my family's future. I also really like school, so college was the obvious choice for me. If I could get paid to be a professional student and take a variety of different classes for the rest of my life, I would do it!

—*JULIE ROBERTS*
EDMOND, OKLAHOMA
UNIVERSITY OF OKLAHOMA

I DECIDED THAT I DIDN'T WANT TO GO TO COLLEGE out of high school. I thought I was great enough and smart enough not to go. But then I realized that people need to go to college in order to operate in the world. And I think you learn not only how to operate in the world as an adult, but you make connections with other people, and you meet people you wouldn't meet someplace else.

—*ANGIE BENIFIELD*
NEW YORK, NEW YORK
HUNTER COLLEGE

A PARENT'S (ULTIMATELY HAPPY) TALE

Our daughter went to an ultra-competitive high school with plenty of ultra-competitive parents in the wings. We parents got the message that applying to college was a blood sport that took brains, guts, strategy, and tactics to succeed. Failure was not an option.

Rachel did not buy into this point of view. She seemed to feel that if she just lived long enough, college would, somehow, inevitably happen to her, without her having to do much planning or choosing. The school (and the culture) had us geared up early in junior year for college reading, plotting, and visiting. Rachel didn't get with the program until almost a year later. She absolutely refused to be packaged: She would not work with a private counselor; she would not read books on how to get into college; she would not do extracurriculars just to pad her résumé; she wrote an unconventional essay (on learning to draw, instead of one on helping to make the world a better place). In other words, she presented herself completely as herself.

The downside: If she had paid attention earlier, she might have decided to apply to certain other, even more prestigious schools, which would have taken advance planning—and she might have been accepted, and that might have been very good for her.

The upside: She applied to seven schools, was accepted at six, and wait-listed at one. She was offered two merit scholarships. She was able to turn to me (repeatedly) and say, "You see? And you said I wouldn't get in anywhere!" Ultimately, she chose to go to a prestigious, very rigorous college, and is happy there so far. It was her decision, and it was a good one. So she can say, "I told you so" as much as she likes.

—ANONYMOUS
NEW YORK, NEW YORK
P CARLETON COLLEGE

THIS IS YOUR MOTHER TALKING

Don't relax when it comes to college admissions. This is the one time when you have to be alert and get this right. This is no joke. This is the rest of your life you're talking about. If you don't get the right education, there will be no more relaxing, because you're going to get stuck in a bad job until you're 65, working most of your adult life. But get it right and you can get a wonderful career that will let you retire on a yacht in the Pacific at 45. See the difference?

—*COLLEEN BAKEY*
FREDERICK, MARYLAND
P *GEORGETOWN UNIVERSITY*

IT IS NEVER TOO EARLY to prepare your child for college. We must prepare our children for college from the moment they begin attending grade school. We must emphasize that education does matter and that going to college is not a choice. There should be an unspoken rule in the house that college is just the transition from high school to the real world. Also, we must give our children the proper tools they need to succeed. These should include providing a good environment to study, showing that we are truly interested in what they do, and encouraging them to *have fun*. Also, offer them help at any time and provide the financial means. Most important, we must be good role models in our everyday life.

—*MERYL SHER*
WESTON, FLORIDA
P *UNIVERSITY OF FLORIDA*

Begin early.

—*NANCY NELSON-DUAC*
GRANBURY, TEXAS
P *GEORGE WASHINGTON UNIVERSITY*

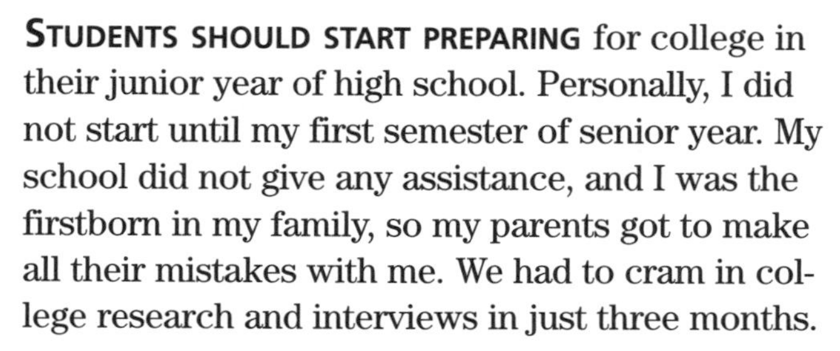

STUDENTS SHOULD START PREPARING for college in their junior year of high school. Personally, I did not start until my first semester of senior year. My school did not give any assistance, and I was the firstborn in my family, so my parents got to make all their mistakes with me. We had to cram in college research and interviews in just three months.

—ELIZABETH BRISTOL
NORTH ATTLEBORO, MASSACHUSETTS
MOUNT HOLYOKE COLLEGE

Look for a school that is nearby but far enough away that your parents can't check in on you on a whim.

—ADAM GUZOWSKI
SOUTH BEND, INDIANA
BALL STATE UNIVERSITY

WE STARTED THINKING about college in my daughter's sophomore year. She was considering a hockey scholarship and started making inquiries into that. We began to research, looked on collegeboard.com, and started going through those college guides.

—CINDY
HERNDON, VIRGINIA
P GEORGE MASON UNIVERSITY

DON'T WAIT UNTIL THE LAST MINUTE to do anything. Get as much done as possible in the summer before your senior year so you can work hard but still enjoy your last year of high school.

—K.F.
BASKING RIDGE, NEW JERSEY
LAFAYETTE COLLEGE

DON'T PROCRASTINATE. I saw a lot of my friends do that, but you're only making things more stressful for yourself in the end. Your application is probably going to seem rushed and you'll have to wait longer to hear whether or not you've been accepted. Applying to colleges is easier if you just get it done as soon as possible.

—ELIZABETH MILLER
DECATUR, GEORGIA
AGNES SCOTT COLLEGE

HEADS UP: FIVE WAYS TO KNOW A COLLEGE RECRUITER IS COMING TO YOU

1. **Get on the mailing lists:** You may receive notice in the mail.

2. **Read the walls:** Colleges send posters to high schools with dates and times of scheduled visits.

3. **Surf the Web:** Colleges will post large-scale public events on their Web pages. You usually do not need invitations to go, although they may request RSVPs.

4. **Visit the guidance office,** college counseling office, or career center and ask the staff for a schedule of visits.

5. **E-mail a specific college you are interested in:** You may not receive an answer, but you can try.

MY MOTHER STARTED THINKING about the whole process a lot earlier than I did. I didn't really consider it until the end of my junior year, and I should have started earlier. In fact, I cut it so close with my application that my parents had to take it down to the 24-hour post office so it could be postmarked by the deadline date. My waiting until the last minute made the whole process more stressful than it had to be.

—*EMILY ROSE*
ATLANTA, GEORGIA
AGNES SCOTT COLLEGE

WHEN TO START?
Most colleges send information by mail only to sophomores, juniors, and seniors. Putting yourself on a college mailing list earlier than that is not necessary.

I HAD HEARD THAT SMALLER COLLEGES and universities offered a more personal experience, which was very important to me. I surfed the Web, requested information about the schools, and interviewed students. My research led me to Marylhurst University and Concordia, both for their small size and close-to-home locations. I chose Marylhurst after meeting with one of their advisers to discuss goals and options. She took the confusion out of scheduling classes by helping me map out a plan that matched my needs. I don't believe I would have received such personal attention at a larger public college or university.

—*SHANNON*
PORTLAND, OREGON
MARYLHURST UNIVERSITY

DON'T BE INTIMIDATED BY COLLEGES. I probably should have applied to the University of Michigan. My grades weren't perfect, and my high school is full of overachievers who didn't get in. I compared myself to my peers and didn't apply. I felt almost like it was too good for me.

—*MINEHAHA FORMAN*
SAN ANTONIO VILLAGE, BELIZE
OAKLAND UNIVERSITY

OTHER SIDE OF THE DESK: ON RECRUITING

Colleges hope to raise the number of applications they receive annually. The goal is to have a wider range of talent from which to choose, and to increase selectivity by admitting a smaller percentage of the pool of applicants. Every year, *all* colleges across the country recruit, both to inform students and parents about their programs and opportunities, and to develop the largest, most talented, and most diverse pool they can. In the fall, AOs can work extremely hard, visiting four to five high schools a day for months straight and making numerous large, public presentations. All schools—even those at the most selective levels—recruit.

DON'T START THE PROCESS TOO EARLY. You might have to make a commitment that you're not ready for. I was only 13 years old entering my freshman year of high school. I think you have to take a little time and allow the child to mature to a certain degree. For me, it worked out because I always knew I wanted to go to UVA, and I liked it. But some of my friends ended up limiting their options and not being happy with the schools they went to.

—*KEN KEEL*
WINCHESTER, VIRGINIA
UNIVERSITY OF VIRGINIA

APPLYING TO SCHOOL and getting ready for college was insanely easy for me because I'm a local *and* I had taken college courses in high school, so it was a direct transfer to my college. If you can take a few courses in advance, I'd recommend it!

—*KYLE*
FT. COLLINS, COLORADO
COLORADO STATE UNIVERSITY

IT'S EASIER TO GET THROUGH THE PROCESS, and get what you want out of it, if you get an early start. I wouldn't want to enter my senior year without any idea of where I wanted to go to college or what I had to do to get there. But starting earlier in your high school years, you have a chance to do things slowly and do them right. I never felt any panic because my parents and I had developed a schedule for when we wanted to get each step in the process done, and we pretty much stuck to it. You can't do that if you wait until the last minute.

—*Bill Lawryk*
Frederick, Maryland
George Washington University

THE WISDOM OF CROWDS

The year 2006 marked an all-time high in the number of high school seniors, according to the National Association for College Admission Counseling. Sixty-five percent of them will enroll in some form of secondary education within a year after graduation.

I STARTED LOOKING ON THE INTERNET my sophomore year and narrowed my search to small to midsized schools with journalism majors. Look at collegeboard.com. It's a very good site. You can see size, location, personal testaments from current students, majors, cost, and reputation from reputable sources (ranking, articles, awards, and so on).

—*Adrienne Lang*
Olathe, Kansas
Texas Christian University

THE FIRST YEAR IN HIGH SCHOOL is when you start to create a record that will play a role in the college admission decision. A picture is being painted by what you do in 9th, 10th, 11th, and 12th grades. Don't think you're going to turn it on in your last year and schools will just ignore the prior years. I had one college tell me that a "D" I got in 9th grade English could have kept me from getting in.

—*Miller Smathers*
Findlay, Ohio

HEADS UP: GETTING ORGANIZED

With all the materials you are receiving and all the information you need to keep straight, how can you keep things organized at home? Here are some tips:

- Make a box or dedicate a desk drawer to college admissions materials.
- For each school, start an individual file or folder.
- Get a wall calendar and mark deadlines for each school on it, including not only application deadlines but financial aid, testing, and recommendation deadlines.
- Work backwards to write in additional personal deadlines. For example, if a teacher recommendation is due on a certain date, mark down a month or two earlier that you need to give your teacher the form to fill out.
- Make a list of all the essay questions you have to answer for all your schools on one page to see what you have to write and where you may have topic overlaps.

HEADS UP: MAKING THE APPLICATION LIST

There are more than 4,000 colleges and universities in the United States. How do you know where to start? Here are the top five resources:

1. **Internet.** Hands down, college and university Web pages have the most information. These days, printed materials from the college are helpful, but they are not necessarily thorough. You can check out a broader range of information online, from academics to clubs to atmosphere to statistics.

2. **University publications.** Definitely check the "send me material" box on the PSAT and PACT—colleges buy names of students they think could be competitive applicants, so you will get information arriving directly to your mailbox. Additionally, fill out forms on other college Web sites requesting information.

3. **Books/videos.** Hopefully, your high school will have a library of college catalogs and information. Spend some time in your college guidance office and ask for help from the staff, volunteers, and students working there.

4. **Parents/Siblings/Close Friends.** People who know you well will be able to suggest places where they think you will thrive. People can be biased, though, so be prepared to take advice with a grain of salt.

5. **College Alumni.** They will share detailed information with you, but again, be careful to always consider the source. They will likely think the place where they attended college is the perfect place for anyone.

I STARTED THINKING about colleges my junior year. My school was really college-oriented, so I was pretty aware of the search process and how it works. It helped that our counselors were really good; they had a list of all of us and made sure everyone applied to at least four places. I liked having my hand held that way.

—*Dana Notestine*
East Point, Georgia
Agnes Scott College

I STARTED LOOKING AT COLLEGES when I was only in the 8th grade. My next-oldest sister was a senior in high school, so I rode on her coattails. I was interested in languages and literature, so I researched what the best schools were in those areas. I recommend doing research and doing it early. Also, look into what the school feels like. Is it a party school or a pressure cooker where everyone has to do so well that no students can enjoy themselves at all? Measure that against your own personality and your own needs.

—*Nancy Poehlmann*
Atlanta, Georgia
Agnes Scott College

JUST THE FACTS

On first contact with a college, don't go overboard: Writing a long letter detailing your many accomplishments and reasons you want information from a school will not make any impact at this stage. Your data (name, address, high school, year of graduation, and possible internal division/school/major) is simply entered into a computer by student workers or clerical staff. The best way is to fill out the school's online form so they can just upload your information.

ASK THE EXPERT

How many applications are too many?

If admissions seem so unpredictable and the safety schools of the past are no longer "safe," you should spread your risk by applying to lots of schools—that seems to be the current thinking. But here's what will soon happen if students apply to more and more schools insincerely and colleges' yield numbers drop: Colleges will be forced to be even harder on applicants and will need to gauge sincerity where they may not have done so before.

Applying to five or six schools is reasonable and expected, with a few true safety schools (including at least one public school) and a few reach schools included. Apply to schools of the same genre (size, atmosphere, location, academic focus) that you want. If you want a small school, focus only on the small ones. If you want quiet, do not apply to urban campuses. Applying to the entire Ivy League is silly—they are quite different schools.

I RESEARCHED SCHOOLS' DANCE programs, and whether or not I could see myself there. Location was also very important to me: I wanted to live in a city, preferably New York. I had made a list of about 10 schools that I was interested in. Then I started applying.

—*Jennifer Keys*
Baltimore, Maryland
New York University

I STARTED LOOKING FOR A COLLEGE about two years after graduating from high school. I decided that working a terrible job wasn't very fun at all!

—*Kevin Butts*
Niles, Michigan
Indiana University

THE PROCESS STARTS WITH the mountains of brochures colleges start sending out after the PSAT. Frankly, those are only good for name recognition; I found word of mouth to be a much more accurate, convenient, and honest source of information. In terms of just seeing what's out there, college search engines (College Board actually puts out a very effective one) are useful in getting started.

—*Emily Wachtel*
Agoura Hills, California
University of California, Los Angeles

I REALLY BEGAN THE PROCESS during my brother's third year of high school, when I was in 8th grade. As a result, I really got a leg up on the process. If you have older siblings, I suggest going on the family trips to tour and check out college campuses. During my junior year, my family and another family went all around California checking out schools. Bring a friend to look at schools: It takes some of the pressure off and makes it more enjoyable.

—*David Lichtenstein*
San Diego, California
University of Southern California

I HAD A BOOK ON THE 100 best schools from *U.S. News & World Report*. Those books are helpful because you find a lot of schools you may not have heard of. I went through that with my mom, looking for what majors the schools offered, whether they were big or small, or whether they were in a city. We started eliminating and got it down to a list of 20. I did more research on those and whittled it down to eight that I applied to.

—*Ashley Little*
Flossmoor, Illinois
Marquette University

NO DIPLOMA? NO PROBLEM

Many colleges, public and private, two-year and four-year, will accept students who have neither graduated from high school nor earned equivalency degrees.

I STARTED VISITING SCHOOLS my sophomore year, but only because my friend's mom was the over-prepared type and I was invited to tag along. I didn't really start learning and looking until the beginning of my senior year. For me, it was just about learning the names of schools and their reputations and then applying to the best ones.

—*Seth*
Sunnyvale, California
University of California, Berkeley

TIP

Make a file for each college that interests you. Include brochures, maps, any important names and contact numbers, deadlines for admission, and financial aid forms.

OUR COLLEGE SEARCH PROCESS was both fun and rewarding. Make it a team effort. My husband and I attended a college prep meeting for parents. The idea is to talk openly and often about after-high-school options, including technical schools, two-year colleges, universities, and military options. Starting early allows for fitting campus visits into vacations without creating anxiety.

—*Nancy Nelson-Duac*
Granbury, Texas
George Washington University

I BEGAN LOOKING AT COLLEGES during my junior year of high school and sent away for information for about 10 schools. That's when I began to get bombarded with information. To narrow my choices down, I went to the schools that offered the specific program I was looking for (in my case, journalism). And I weighed the pluses and minuses of my other options, such as whether the college was liberal or conservative, whether or not the school had an honors program, whether or not it offered scholarships, and its size.

—*Jason Torreano*
Lockport, New York
State University of New York, Brockport

I STARTED LOOKING AT COLLEGES as early as 8th grade; my parents took me to Stanford to try to motivate me early. However, my college search really started early in my junior year. We started to travel the country looking at schools to narrow them down, and we continued to do so through the first semester of my senior year.

—*Coral A. Schneider*
Cherry Hills Village, Colorado
University of Southern California

MY FIRST STEP WAS TO FIND the universities that offered programs I was interested in. My final decision was actually based on laziness. The school I chose for my undergraduate degree is only one block from my parents' home.

—*Natalia Jimenez*
Medellin, Colombia
Indiana University

BRIDGING SCHOOL WITH THE GAP YEAR

Although taking a year off in between high school and college is not as prevalent here as it is in the UK and Europe, there are a number of excellent gap year programs in the United States. It can be a very maturing experience, which often translates to an academic advantage. Check out these Web sites to learn more:

- **www.gap-year.com**
- **www.yearoutgroup.org**
- **www.leapnow.org/home.htm**
- **www.bunac.org**
- **www.interimprograms.com/sampleprograms/index.asp**
- **www.transitionsabroad.com/listings/work/shortterm/gap_year_jobs_abroad.shtml**
- **www.traveltree.co.uk/pages/gap-year-programs.asp**

NOT ALL COLLEGE CATALOGS are the same. Sarah Lawrence College expressed its unique philosophy on every page. My daughter kept an extra copy in her bag. It gave in-depth information far beyond course descriptions. She could see more clearly who they were. She understood why she would be so happy there.

—*MICKIE MANDEL*
RIVERDALE, NEW YORK
P SARAH LAWRENCE COLLEGE

It helps if you have learned to take responsibility for yourself at an early age and throughout your high school career.

—*TRINA COOKE*
STRUTHERS, OHIO

WE STARTED TALKING about different colleges during my daughter's junior year and she attended a day for high school students at Kansas University that year. I think that this timeline was about right. Earlier would have given us too much time to think about it, but later would have rushed the process too much.

—*JAYNE ROBERTS*
EDMOND, OKLAHOMA
P UNIVERSITY OF OKLAHOMA

THE FIRST TIME I started thinking about college was when schools started sending stuff to me. They all looked good in the brochures. Then it was a matter of thinking, "I like how this looks. Does it have the program I want? What does it cost? What are the scholarship opportunities?"

—*JULIE COLLINS*
DES MOINES, IOWA
DRAKE UNIVERSITY

SAT, ACT, AP Classes: Studying & Scoring High

The new SAT debuted in 2005, with a new format that challenges students to prepare for it in a different way. The test is just one determining factor that colleges use in an alphabet of academic qualifications: your GPA, your ACT and SAT II scores, your AP or IB classes. But it's a big one: Schools that receive many thousands of applications often make their first cut based on test scores. We asked others how they prepared for tests and tough classes, and here are their stories and tips.

SAT AND ACT: six letters that every high school student dreads! Most important when studying: Learn your weaknesses. If you are really good at math, work on the reading and logic sections, and vice versa. It is important to know what skills you lack and hone those for these tests.

—ANDREW J. BURKE
CINCINNATI, OHIO
UNIVERSITY OF CINCINNATI

DON'T BE AFRAID TO ASK FOR HELP! I'M GLAD I DID.

—DANIELLA KANAL
PITTSBURGH, PENNSYLVANIA
STERN COLLEGE

- Know your strengths and weaknesses and get help where you need it.
- Find the test prep that best suits your needs and abilities.
- Practice, practice, practice—the more tests you take, the better you'll get at it.
- Maintain perspective: Testing ability is only one aspect of your applicant profile.
- Relax: High anxiety won't help you test well.

TAKE THE PSAT AS A SOPHOMORE to prepare for the SAT, which will be given during your junior year. That way, you are ahead of the game. I learned so much more about the actual SATs by taking the PSAT than from any of the study guides I read.

—*TRINA COOKE*
STRUTHERS, OHIO

I LEARNED THAT THE SAT means nothing. A few years after taking it, I do not even recall my scores, nor are they important, nor did they predict my success thus far in college. Try to do well, of course, but you aren't labeled by your SAT score.

—*NICOLE SPENCE*
WYCKOFF, NEW JERSEY
EMORY UNIVERSITY

MY FRIEND AND I WERE on spring break during our junior year of high school and came up with the terrible idea to take the test while we were in Florida. We stayed up until 5 a.m. the night before and walked in after about three hours of sleep. Neither of us had taken classes or prepared in any way. I pretty much stared into space during the entire test. I got a decent score, but I could've done better if I'd been better prepared.

—*SCOTT COOLBAUGH*
KNOXVILLE, TENNESSEE
UNIVERSITY OF TENNESSEE

Take the ACTs. I took the SATs three times, and did so much better taking the ACTs once.

—*ADAM KRESSEL*
MIAMI, FLORIDA
CORNELL UNIVERSITY

I'M NOT A STRESSFUL TEST TAKER. The only way I prepped for the SAT was with a computer program and a book. I did fine, but I wish I had been a little more stressed about it. When I got my scores back, I cried, but I still didn't change my work ethic. If I could do it over, I would have had a tutor. It would have helped my score.

—*MARY KATE TAULANE*
HUNTINGDON VALLEY, PENNSYLVANIA
LOYOLA COLLEGE

YOU NEED TO BE REALISTIC about your strengths and weaknesses. And if you're not, hopefully you will have someone close to you who can help you to see where you need tutoring. I was smart enough to know that I wasn't going to do well on the English portion of the SAT and got myself some tutoring before I ever took the test and screwed it up. You have to figure out where you need the help, and then be a big enough person to admit it and to seek it out.

—*KEN KEEL*
WINCHESTER, VIRGINIA
UNIVERSITY OF VIRGINIA

TAKE THE PSAT INSTEAD OF just jumping right into the SAT. If I had the experience of taking the PSAT, it would have raised my score by 100 points.

—*MARTY MADDOCK*
NEWARK, DELAWARE
UNIVERSITY OF DELAWARE

"I did horribly on my SAT. What did I learn? Use the book, pay for the course, and pay attention to your math and grammar classes in school! And it's never too early to start preparing."

—*WILLIAM WATTS*
BERKELEY, CALIFORNIA
UNIVERSITY OF CALIFORNIA, BERKELEY

FIND A GOOD TEACHER. My teacher for the Kaplan SAT prep course was a young graduate from Lehigh University. He made it fun to come to class twice a week and encouraged the class to do the work: If we did, he would tell us a story about his adventures in college. Finding a class that was fun encouraged me to participate, and doing the work is what caused my scores to go up. I felt relaxed when I went to the test because I felt the class prepared me to the best of my ability.

—*ROB FEHN*
BASKING RIDGE, NEW JERSEY
LAFAYETTE COLLEGE

HEADS UP: THE NEW SAT

The new SAT is a longer test, which means a bigger fatigue factor. That might be one reason why scores are down, according to college admissions consultant Betsy F. Woolf, who suggests getting detailed reports on your scores from the College Board. "Everything is dollars and cents," she says. "It costs money to take a test: it costs money to get the results." But she feels it's worth spending the extra money to see how you did. The Question and Answer service provides your test questions for the SAT Reasoning test, the correct answers, scoring instructions, and the opportunity to order your answer sheet.

You get the type of question, its level of difficulty, and whether you answered correctly, incorrectly, or left it blank. You can even ask them to go back and hand-score your test, "for another fee, of course," she adds.

You can also ask them not to score your test or to cancel your score, up until the Wednesday after taking the test, if you don't feel you did well. "I don't encourage this" says Ms. Woolf, "because many students think they bombed when actually, they didn't."

WHAT IS AP?

AP (Advanced Placement) courses are advanced, college-level courses offered in high schools. There are exams for each of these courses, graded on a scale of 1 to 5, from which students can possibly gain college credit. Colleges have individual policies on what test scores are acceptable for credit, if any. Top schools accept only a 5 for credit. In general, students competing for places at top universities are taking these courses and scoring 5 on the exams.

GIVE YOURSELF ENOUGH TIME to examine what type of studying works best for you. If your initial method doesn't meet your expectations on your first test results, try a different method for the second time. The nice thing about the ACT is that you can submit whatever score is best.

—SCOTT G.
CHESTERFIELD, MISSOURI
UNIVERSITY OF ILLINOIS

I TOOK A COURSE AT KAPLAN TEST PREP. The great thing about a course is not just that it gives you strategies you might otherwise miss out on, but it also forces you into a regimented study schedule, which ensures that you'll actually do the work. It's also a good way to meet people who are in the same boat and form study groups.

—LAUREN ELIZABETH LEAHY
DALLAS, TEXAS
SOUTHERN METHODIST UNIVERSITY

I DIDN'T STUDY FOR THE SAT AT ALL. I just went in and took it once at the beginning of my senior year. I ended up doing quite well on it. The test that I really focused on was the ACT instead of the SAT. I started preparing for it, and taking it, my sophomore year in high school. To prepare for it, I bought a bunch of practice test booklets. I would make myself take those practice tests with a "test setting" mind-set. It worked for me.

—*KELLY PARMET*
HOUSTON, TEXAS
SOUTHWESTERN UNIVERSITY

I STARTED PREPARING FOR THE SATs by reviewing vocabulary words and taking a math class at my high school that focused on the types of math problems found on the SATs. After taking the SATs once at the beginning of my junior year and not being happy with my score, I got a private tutor for both the math and reading sections. The math class and the tutor were the best at helping me raise my SAT score.

—*JENNA ISZAUK*
MONROEVILLE, PENNSYLVANIA
OHIO UNIVERSITY

SAT math questions are arranged in ascending order of difficulty. Don't spend too much time on the first questions; you'll probably answer them easily.

—*B.T.*
WILMINGTON, DELAWARE
UNIVERSITY OF DELAWARE

THE SAT SUBJECT TESTS

In addition to the new SAT, some universities require SAT Subject Tests. These tests help admissions committees assess how much you are learning in your classes—the SAT reflects math and English, but the SAT Subject Tests address other subject areas.

THE NEW SAT: IT REALLY IS DIFFERENT

I'M GOING TO BE AN ENGLISH MAJOR so I wasn't happy when I found out the new SAT has a heavier emphasis on math and that the math is more advanced. But the one good tip my counselor gave me was to remember that it only counts for 10 percent of the final score. So don't get yourself so worked up about the math that you forget about everything else. In the big picture it's not going to make or break your final score.

—*ANONYMOUS*
BROWNSVILLE, MARYLAND
UNIVERSITY OF MARYLAND

WHILE TOURING A COLLEGE CAMPUS, I received some of the most important information regarding taking the math SAT II. A tour guide informed me that although the Math 2C test was harder, it is scaled much greater than the Math 1C test is. This means that you can answer more problems incorrectly and do just as well. He pointed out that if you completely miss 10 out of the 50 items on the test, you can still get a 700 (which is all you really need, I believe), and so it was more important to focus and do well on the first 40 and skip the rest if need be. As a result of using this tactic, I got a 710 on the Math 2C test.

—*DAVID LICHTENSTEIN*
SAN DIEGO, CALIFORNIA
UNIVERSITY OF SOUTHERN CALIFORNIA

START EARLY. You will probably not use the score from your sophomore year, but the more times you take the test, the better you will do. Use the tutorial books, too. They really helped me in subjects I struggled in, such as science reasoning.

—STEFANIE FRY
KNOXVILLE, TENNESSEE
UNIVERSITY OF TENNESSEE

> "Make sure you know where the test site is *before* the day of the test. I've heard way too many horror stories about getting lost on the way to the test site on the morning of the test."

—CARRIE BERTOLOZZI
CHAPEL HILL, NORTH CAROLINA
UNIVERSITY OF NORTH CAROLINA

YOU CAN DEFINITELY RAISE YOUR SAT scores by more than 100 points: I raised my math score by more than 150 points. I wasn't happy with my score the first time I took the test, and then I studied a lot with books. I set a goal of getting above a certain score in math and I kept going at it until I got it. I wanted to prove to myself that I could do it. I was in heaven when I got the scores back. That was more fun than getting into my school. I just remember walking around so happy, smiling all the time.

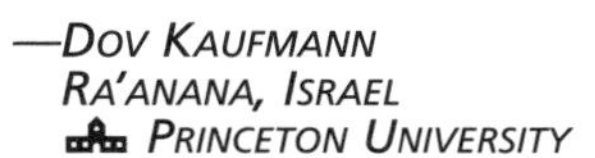
—DOV KAUFMANN
RA'ANANA, ISRAEL
PRINCETON UNIVERSITY

I THINK TOO MUCH STRESS AND EMPHASIS is put on the SATs and getting into the Ivy League. Really, anyone can make a great academic and social experience out of any school.

—*JILLIAN NADELL*
GREENSBORO, NORTH CAROLINA
UNIVERSITY OF NORTH CAROLINA

I WASN'T SATISFIED WITH MY SCORES, so I got the name of a private tutor from my friend who had raised his scores on the ACT. After a month or two of being tutored by this guy, I took the test. I got my scores back and they had gone up significantly. Get a private tutor: It really benefits you.

—*ANGELA FRIEDMAN*
PEORIA, ILLINOIS
BRADLEY UNIVERSITY

BE PREPARED FOR ANYTHING. I had to take my SAT partly in the dark because the school lost power. But my score was OK, and I didn't want to go through that again, so I didn't retake it.

—*ANONYMOUS*
BREMEN, INDIANA
INDIANA UNIVERSITY

I ENROLLED IN AN SAT PREP CLASS and it was a complete waste of money. I paid almost $1,000 for the course, "taught" by a guy who barely spoke English. The teacher just gave us practice tests; he didn't go over anything unless we asked about it. He would just sit there and wait for us to finish the test. What a waste! If I did it again, I would try to learn with a private tutor instead of taking a class. Ask around and see if anyone has recommendations.

—*BARAK KRENGEL*
DALLAS, TEXAS
UNIVERSITY OF KANSAS

Use the book *10 Real SATs* and just keep doing practice problems. Also, learn a lot of vocabulary words.

—*ALLISON LEVE*
BALTIMORE, MARYLAND
NEW YORK UNIVERSITY

THE FIRST TIME I TOOK THE SAT, I was scared: I thought if I didn't get a certain score, I wouldn't be accepted to my top schools. I did decently, but I wasn't satisfied. I ended up taking it a second time, this time feeling that I had nothing to lose, since colleges only look at your best score. My score went up considerably, even though I didn't prepare any more than I did the first time. I attribute it to being a lot calmer when I was taking it. I didn't feel rushed, the words didn't blur together in the reading section like the first time.

—KATHERINE BELL
STANFORD, CALIFORNIA
STANFORD UNIVERSITY

I TOOK THE SATs TWICE, doing significantly better the second time. I did not study for the second one, but rather I just had the confidence of knowing what to expect. Confidence is the key with these tests; it is very important to not worry about it for too long. When people would try to talk to me about being nervous about the test, I would always change the topic.

—NATHANIEL COHEN
WEST HARTFORD, CONNECTICUT
NEW YORK UNIVERSITY

Don't freak out. I exercised a lot the week of the test. I slept well, and the day of the test I did the best that I could.

—HANNAH ASSADI
SCOTTSDALE, ARIZONA
COLUMBIA COLLEGE

SHOULD YOU TAKE THE SUBJECT TEST?

Deciding whether to take the SAT Subject Tests depends on where you want to go. Most colleges don't require these tests, which measure knowledge in specific areas. But more competitive programs want to see scores from two separate areas, along with your regular SAT. Several Ivies want to see scores from three tests.

ASK THE EXPERT

How important are test scores to AOs?

High schools and their grading processes are not created equal, so AOs need to look at national testing to help gauge talent on a single, measurable scale. A student can earn an A by cramming for a test, as well from learning in class. AOs want to know who has been learning. They understand that testing can be particularly challenging to some people, and that family income and access to test preparation influences students' scores. Desirable students may not need the top scores if they can score well enough to show that they can do the work at the college, but students from major "feeder" areas for colleges will likely need strong scores.

YOU CAN'T OVEREMPHASIZE the importance of your score on the SAT for getting into the college you want. Many schools now say that the test is not as important to them as it once was, but it still carries a lot of weight.

—*TED SASKIN*
CAMPBELL, OHIO
KENT STATE UNIVERSITY

• • • • • • • •

I TOOK THE SATs THREE TIMES. I was never happy with my scores. The only time I was satisfied was after I did the CD-ROM prep course. I didn't believe it was going to be useful, but it was. What really helped me was the way they focused on test strategies, such as that the math questions are ordered in increasing magnitude and how you should pick one in the middle and work your way up or down. That helped.

—*DAVID*
NEWARK, DELAWARE
VILLANOVA UNIVERSITY

Bring extra pencils. When I took the SAT, I lost my only pencil and had to ask the weird girl next to me for hers.

—*NATHANIEL COHEN*
WEST HARTFORD, CONNECTICUT
NEW YORK UNIVERSITY

I STARTED SAT PREP THE SUMMER before my junior year. I bought a book called *10 Real SATs* and started taking some of the practice tests whenever I had time. I took my first SAT the November of my junior year, and then I took it a second time in May and a third time in June before my senior year of high school. The practice SATs really helped out and I improved my writing score by 30 points. There are some SAT-prep courses that I could have taken, but they cost about a grand for the classes alone, and the book cost $20!

—*Julieta A. Grinffiel*
Dallas, Texas
Southern Methodist University

I TOOK A HALF-SEMESTER-LONG COURSE at my school to prepare before I took the test. It met once a week for three hours and we took practice tests and discussed test-taking strategies. We worked out of a big SAT workbook-type thing, and we had practice tests to do for homework as well. Take the course close to the test date: The second time I took the test, I performed worse than I did the first time because I hadn't really prepared well and I'd forgotten simple little strategies that I'd picked up during the class.

—*Carrie Bertolozzi*
Chapel Hill, North Carolina
University of North Carolina

GET YOUR HANDS ON AS MANY PRACTICE TESTS as possible, starting a few weeks before the SAT. It is best to stop preparing two to three days before the test date. This deadline allows you to calm down and relax before taking the test.

—*Catherine Howard*
New Orleans, Louisiana
Southern Methodist University

GRADES AS A CRYSTAL BALL

Less than 14 percent of students with high school grade averages of C or lower earn a two- or four-year college degree.

AS FAR AS SAT-PREP CLASSES GO, you need to know the levels of the class you've signed up for. I was in a much more advanced class than I should've been in, and it was hard to keep up. You may want to opt for a lower-level class so you feel as if you're at the same pace as the others practicing with you.

—*Zach Handler*
St. Louis, Missouri
Brandeis University

"Don't carpool to your SAT exam. It's hard to see a friend walk out at the end of the test and feel as if you have to rush to get out and get a lift home."

—*Lauren Sher*
Gainesville, Florida
University of Florida

I TOOK BOTH THE SAT AND ACT twice in an attempt to better my score. In both cases, when I received the higher score, I had been with friends the night before at a theater cast party, relaxing and having fun. The best advice I can give is just relax about it. Yes, it's important, but keep in mind that it's just words, bubbles to fill in, and a couple of pencils. It does not and cannot truly define you as a person.

—*Jessica Pauley*
Chillicothe, Ohio
University of Cincinnati

ASK THE EXPERT

Now that schools can see that you took the test several times to get a higher score, does that count against you?

AOs expect students to take the tests a few times. However, at some point, scores do not change dramatically. When testing becomes its own major extracurricular activity without significant reward, stop! You are simply wasting your time and it is sad to see. Multiple tests will never count against you, but you should find your own balance for own peace of mind.

THE FIRST TIME I TOOK MY ACT, I had prepared with Web sites and CD-ROMs. I went in with the motivation to do better than my three older brothers (I did), and the knowledge that this was my first try, so I could relax. The second time I took it, I was very ill and scored one point lower, even after taking a class to prepare.

—*ADRIENNE LANG*
OLATHE, KANSAS
TEXAS CHRISTIAN UNIVERSITY

I DID TERRIBLY ON MY SATS! I had the same score three times in a row. The thing is, I don't think this test measured my intelligence. Ultimately, I got a scholarship to a good school and did well. I didn't stress too much about my score, and it was fine. Take it for what it is—it doesn't measure your intelligence.

—*KALPANA*
OLD BRIDGE, NEW JERSEY
RUTGERS UNIVERSITY

WITH SO MUCH HYPE ABOUT THE SATS, the whole process seems much scarier than it actually is. Like most other students in my grade, I was nervous and thought that the results would weigh heavily on my college acceptance. Although some state schools used the grades as cutoff points for different amounts for scholarships, it turned out not to be as important as I had assumed. I promised myself I would be proud as long as I tried my hardest. And I got the help I needed in my weaker subjects. In the end, I was very happy with my score.

—*MELISSA BERMAN*
MANALAPAN, NEW JERSEY
MUHLENBERG COLLEGE

BEFORE THE MORNING OF THE EXAM, make sure you have lots of pens and pencils, and a calculator with an extra battery. If you like using a timer, bring one. And if you're taking the test for the first time, just keep reminding yourself that you can take it many more times.

—*DANA*
LAWRENCE, NEW YORK
HARVARD UNIVERSITY

WHAT IS IB?

The IB (International Baccalaureate) is a challenging, international, standardized curriculum replicated in all countries around the world. The IB requires a specific set of courses, including a senior-year thesis, and several tests throughout the process, scored on a scale of 1 to 7. Colleges and universities may grant college credit based on the test scores. The IB is becoming more popular in U.S. high schools as an alternative to the AP curriculum for top students, but it is still not widely available.

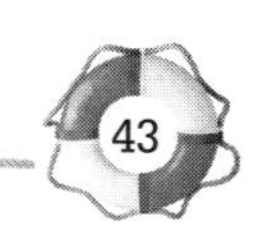

I GOT HELP AT A SYLVAN PROGRAM. The help they give you is great, if you are willing to do the work! Thirty minutes a day is really all you need.

—*JENNIFER KEYS*
BALTIMORE, MARYLAND
NEW YORK UNIVERSITY

"Those courses they offer for the SATs might sound like a waste of time, but they're not. My score went up 150 points after taking one and I had a pretty decent score already. That definitely helped my chances."

—*WILLIAM ALVAREZ*
LYNDHURST, NEW JERSEY
RUTGERS UNIVERSITY

FAMILIARIZE YOURSELF WITH the types of questions and frequent topics covered, then just relax and do your best. A good idea is to take the test your junior year. That way, if you score well, you're set; if you need to retest, you have time. I started SAT prep my sophomore year of high school, working on vocabulary, general math concepts, and logic exercises. I worked with two of the available prep kits on the market; taking the practice tests relieved a lot of my stress about taking the actual SATs.

—*AMANDA NELSON-DUAC*
ST. AUGUSTINE, FLORIDA
GEORGE WASHINGTON UNIVERSITY

I DID TONS OF PREP FOR THE SAT; I got a book and did drills and practice SATs. I don't think it helped much. In addition to the SATs, I took the ACT, because it has less weight on the math section. With the ACT, I basically went in cold and scored higher, comparatively, than I did on the SAT. The ACT was the one I submitted to the schools.

—*Dahvid Castillo-Reminick*
Bronxvile, Florida
Sarah Lawrence College

Don't stress. The night before my test, I relaxed and watched movies, and I did much better than the time before.

—*Janet*
Los Angeles, California
University of California, Los Angeles

I HAD A COUNSELOR TELL ME that it was more beneficial to get a lower grade in a tougher class than a higher grade in an easy class, which really surprised me. I learned not to be afraid to get a lower grade in a more challenging course. While the ideal is getting the best grade possible in the most difficult class, colleges will be impressed with your willingness to stretch your mind rather than just protect your GPA. And don't think they can't tell. They know when you have put it on cruise control and when you're still pushing yourself.

—*Sam Ulmer*
Newark, Delaware
University of Delaware

I NEVER THOUGHT A CLASS would really help my SAT score. The first time I took it, I got a 1220. Then I went to a place where I could get one-on-one tutoring. I spent about five to eight hours with this lady, one hour a week, doing problems with her. I didn't think it would help much, but my score went up from 1220 to 1280 and then 1300 the third time around. So that really helped me a lot.

—*Marek Dudziak*
Bayonne, New Jersey
Loyola College

PREPARER EXTRAORDINAIRE

Whether reading or in a conversation, whenever I encountered a word that I didn't recognize, I would take the time to look it up in the dictionary. Then I would attempt to use that word in daily conversation in the future. This habit allowed me to further develop my vocabulary, to write on a more advanced level, and to improve my SAT writing scores. As with any other test, get a good night's sleep the night before and eat a healthy breakfast. My dad always fixes me eggs; he says it's good brain food! Also, make sure that the proctor has a clock placed in easy view so that you can keep track of the time. Come prepared with your number 2 pencils, a calculator, a watch (if you think it's necessary), a healthy snack, and water, so you won't be stressed the morning of the test. If you easily get cold in classrooms, bring a sweatshirt so that the room temperature is not a distraction. Personally, I bundle up before every test. While taking tests, I attempt to focus all of my attention on the task at hand by blocking out and eliminating as many distractions as possible. Remember to use the restroom before you begin!

—*Brittany Ryan*
Dallas, Texas
University of Oklahoma

I took the SAT at my high school. The familiar setting calmed my nerves.

—*Whitney Tritt*
Atlanta, Georgia
Wake Forest University

In the fall of my junior year I started going to an SAT tutor who prepped me in the math and verbal sections, as well as the writing. It was very helpful, as the tutor picked up on my individual areas of weakness and helped me remedy them. I ended up increasing my score by almost 200 points. I imagine that an SAT class would not have helped me as effectively in that way.

—*Sam*
Palo Alto, California
Stanford University

Get some sleep before the SAT. I only took it once, and I fell asleep halfway through. As you can imagine, my scores weren't as good as I hoped. I mean, I did OK. But I was nervous about them for a while, because I had been drooling on my test.

—*Jessamyn Goshom*
Washington, D.C.
University of Maryland, College Park

PREP AND SAVE

Collected advice about preparing for the SAT:

- Stress can sometimes hurt SAT scores more than a lack of academic knowledge. Familiarity with the test can help test takers calm down.
- Take advantage of test-preparation tools such as the free timed practice tests, complete with monitors, run by Kaplan and the Princeton Review.
- According to one expert, most high school students can "do as well as they need to" using Web-based test prep, or prep sessions offered through their schools. The exception would be "the most ultra-competitive colleges."

I'M THE TYPE OF STUDENT who needs someone pushing me to study for an exam like the SAT. I needed someone on my case to make sure I did practice tests to prepare.

—*Nicole Spence*
Wyckoff, New Jersey
Emory University

"On the morning of the test, eat breakfast. Take deep breaths. It was good to know that I had something fun I was doing that afternoon. I was looking forward to it. I was going to get through this and there would be life after the SATs."

—*Caroline*
Hamilton, Massachusetts
Brown University

FOR THE WRITING PART, you have to get their attention right off the bat. You need a really clear opening paragraph, including a clear, concise thesis statement. If you lose the people who grade these tests at the start, you'll likely never get them back. Take extra time, if necessary, but come out of the gate strong. If you don't, it won't matter how you finish the essay.

—*Anonymous*
Brownsville, Maryland
University of Maryland

SPECIAL CIRCUMSTANCES

FOR ME, THE SATS WERE THE MOST DIFFICULT PART of the college application process. The first time I took the SATs, I was right in the middle of Lyme disease treatment. I had an IV in my arm. I had to get up very early on the day of the test, and I wasn't used to doing that. It took a long time to think about things, and I had to muddle through. My score wasn't bad, but if I hadn't been sick I would have done a lot better. I'd suggest that anyone who's sick look into special accommodations. I didn't do that because I didn't want to be different. I was still at the beginning of my illness and was still coming to the realization that I needed special help. I made it a lot harder on myself than it needed to be.

—*K.E.*
HERNDON, VIRGINIA
GEORGE MASON UNIVERSITY

• • • • • • • •

TO ACCOMMODATE MY DAUGHTER'S ADHD, I tried to talk to her about the true value of the SATs, so she could approach them with less anxiety. The true value means that she's good at taking the test; that's the only thing it tells. This wouldn't be a true measure of whether she was smart or would succeed in college. In preparation for the SATs, I had an SAT tutor to help her. When it came time to take the test, she was allowed to take untimed tests. You have to go through the guidance counselor to do this. As it turned out, she applied to a school—Sarah Lawrence College—that asked for test results but didn't put a lot of emphasis on them.

—*ANONYMOUS*
PHILADELPHIA, PENNSYLVANIA
P SARAH LAWRENCE COLLEGE

TAKE THE CLEP tests (College Level Examination Program) for any classes you think you have any chance of testing out of. It will save you a lot of money. It gives you the opportunity to take tests on subjects you already have knowledge of to earn college credits. And the tests are cheap, about $60 per test. I CLEP-ed out of French 1 and 2 and earned six college credits for one test! That saved me literally thousands of dollars. And if you flunk it, so what? You're only out $60.

—C.L.
NEW MIDDLETOWN, OHIO
YOUNGSTOWN STATE UNIVERSITY

I TOOK AN SAT PREP COURSE the summer before junior year and followed it up with individual tutoring sessions before each SAT that I took. I also took many practice SATs through the tutoring center I used. After those tests, we'd go over my mistakes.

—ERICA ROGGEN
SYRACUSE, NEW YORK
SYRACUSE UNIVERSITY

SAT SCORES DON'T MEASURE YOUR INTELLIGENCE. They are a measure of how much money you or your parents were able to spend on classes and private tutors. Since you have to do well on them to get into college, I highly recommend spending as much as you can for help. I used Kaplan and the Princeton Review, and I had private tutors. They teach you tricks that help you during the test. For example, they teach you ways to know the answers to a section without reading the entire passage.

—ANONYMOUS
LOS ANGELES, CALIFORNIA
UNIVERSITY OF CALIFORNIA, LOS ANGELES

SOMETHING TO CONSIDER

How important are your standardized test scores? Sixty percent of colleges assign "considerable importance" to them, according to a survey by the National Association for College Admission Counseling.

I WISH I'D SPENT MORE TIME studying for the SAT and the ACT, and I wish I'd known a little more about the SAT subject tests. I just randomly chose U.S. history for the subject test and didn't score so well on it. I still scored fairly well on the SAT, but it would have helped if I'd studied more and brought my score up, even if it was just by 50 points—even 50 points is a pretty big deal for most colleges.

—Dane Skilbred
Saint Paul, Minnesota
Santa Clara University

KEEP IN MIND THAT SCHOOLS look not only at the grades you receive but also the classes you receive them in. Therefore, it is important that you challenge yourself with honors and Advanced Placement (AP) classes that are on par with college-freshman-level courses. As much as I wanted to take the easy way out, that's what I did. And I actually scored better than I thought. You don't know what you can accomplish until you put your mind to it.

—C.D.
New Middletown, Ohio
Youngstown State University

A NUMBER TWO PENCIL AND A STICK OF GUM

Research has found that chewing gum stimulates certain areas of the brain, which may have a relationship to reducing tension. Furthermore, one study conducted in 2002 showed that chewing gum appeared to improve people's ability to retain and retrieve information.

HEADS UP: ACT VS SAT

The ACT is more about achievement and what you've learned in school; the SAT's focus is more on reasoning and aptitude. Most colleges will accept either ACTs or SATs.

The big difference: The College Board will send all SAT test scores to your college of choice, no matter how many times you take the test, and they will generally look at the best results from each test. But you can take the ACT in May and June, and just send in the test that you feel shows you to your best advantage.

Some schools, such as Holy Cross and Drew University, have gone SAT-optional, and both have seen a significant spike in applications. This is ideal for students who get good grades, but are not good test takers. Colleges understand this; they primarily look at students' GPAs and the courses they have taken. This option often gives the school a greater pool of really good students, and in turn they can be more selective. The irony is that most students send in their test scores anyway.

MY BEST FRIEND WENT TO A DIFFERENT high school than I did. Since we didn't see each other every day, whenever we got together, we were always out of control. The second time I took my SAT, she happened to be in the same room with me, since our last names are right next to each other in the alphabet. Just being in the same room with her threw off my concentration because we couldn't stop laughing at each other. Needless to say, I scored below my first SAT results. Moral of the story: Don't take the SATs in the same room as your best friend, because you won't be able to take *anything* seriously.

—*JESSICA*
SARATOGA, CALIFORNIA
UNIVERSITY OF SOUTHERN CALIFORNIA

The key is to do lots of practice tests, make flash cards, and get a good night's sleep before the day of the test.

—*ELANA SYRTASH*
TORONTO, ONTARIO
STERN COLLEGE

YOUNG BUT SMART

Surprised that your AO is a 21-year-old, newly minted college graduate and not a Ph.D. in education? Don't start to think that these AOs are friends. They should still be addressed as "Ms." or "Mr." and be taken seriously. Attempts at friendship with an AO will not get you admitted: AOs all work for the dean, and they see through the flattery.

I TOOK THE ACT and prepared for it by taking the classes. When I got my score, I opened the letter, fell to the ground, and burst into tears. I had gotten a 21. I remember saying, "I will never get into college with this score." I retook the test and got a whopping 23, but at that point I realized that I had the GPA, the activities, the grades, the recommendation letters, and the essays to prove that I just can't do tests, but I'm still a smart person. And I was right! I got into all three colleges that I applied for. I realized the ACT cannot judge your intelligence.

—*Angela Massini*
Chicago, Illinois
Butler University

THE SAT RULES SAY NO FOOD DURING THE TEST, but I can't do without food for even a minute. Since I've broken every food law on earth, I naturally brought food into the test. My advice, though, is to bring something that doesn't melt. I brought chocolate, but when I reached into my pocket to get it, it was completely melted. I had to keep licking my fingers throughout the test.

—*Janet*
Los Angeles, California
University of California, Los Angeles

First Impressions: On Essays, Applications & Interviews

It's impossible for admissions officers to meet even a majority of the students who want to get into their schools. That's why the application essay plays such a pivotal role: It's the school's first impression of the student—a window into the student's life and a crystal ball that reveals the person's potential. In this chapter, we asked college students for essay advice and topics. We also sought their tips on filling out those tedious applications, as well as on acing an interview with a college admissions officer.

DON'T PROCRASTINATE. Know the deadlines beforehand and work in advance. Try to send out your applications by the end of October so you can focus on scholarships and last-minute things in November and December.

—*Sarah Bormel*
Baltimore, Maryland
Boston University

BE YOURSELF. IF YOU ARE FUNNY, WRITE A FUNNY ESSAY; IF YOU ARE SERIOUS, WRITE A SERIOUS ESSAY.

—*Dave Cross*
Campbell, Ohio

- Keep a list of everything you've done so you won't leave something out.
- Let your personality shine through in your essay.
- Switch roles: Look at your applications and essay as if you were the reader.
- Find fresh eyes to look over your application, both for errors and for impact.
- Don't underestimate the power or importance of a face-to-face interview.

Apply online. Some online applications do not require a fee.

—*Phyllis Briskman Stanfield*
Pittsburgh, Pennsylvania
Washington and Jefferson College

Keep a list of your activities, awards, jobs, and volunteer service. It is too difficult to remember everything that you did for the last four years. You want to put your best foot forward and it is frustrating to feel that you could have included something else.

—*Jayne Roberts*
Edmond, Oklahoma
University of Oklahoma

Start off with something that will draw the reader in. These people are reading thousands upon thousands of essays. If yours starts off interesting, you have a better chance.

—*Dana*
Lawrence, New York
Harvard University

THE COMMON APPLICATION is a high school student's best friend. All of the schools that I applied to were Common Application schools. I focused on one idea and really got to concentrate on my application and make it the best that it could be.

—*Rob Fehn*
Basking Ridge, New Jersey
Lafayette College

“Your essay is your time to shine. The people looking at this essay have probably never met you. You need to paint them a picture of yourself. Tell them everything.”

—*Kathrine Novak*
Shelby Township, Michigan
Central Michigan University

THERE IS NOTHING WRONG with blowing one's horn, especially when everyone else vying for a spot at the same school is doing just that. An application is no time to show how modest you can be. This is a time to say, “Look at me, look what I have done, and look at what I can accomplish.” The people who write your recommendation letters are going to focus on the best and the brightest aspects of your personality and high school career, and you should do the same to really cement what those individuals have stated.

—*Catherine Howard*
New Orleans, Louisiana
Southern Methodist University

A GOOD WAY TO AVOID or lessen stress is to become as organized as possible. When application time rolls around (or even beforehand), you should write a list of everything you've been involved with in high school. That way, a résumé shouldn't be hard to compile when the time comes. Check out schools' Web sites. Find out the criteria colleges use for acceptance, so nothing is a surprise. And when you have an idea of whom you would want to write your recommendations, ask them; it's never too early.

—Katie
New York, New york
New York University

• • • • • • • •

THE STRESSFUL PART WAS FILLING OUT all of the applications, especially since each one was different and asked different questions. If possible, you should try to write one essay that can be adapted to fit multiple questions for different applications.

—Allison Leve
Baltimore, Maryland
New York University

Take your time with your applications. Make them look nice and include things that may impress the reader.

—Sarah Bormel
Baltimore, Maryland
Boston University

• • • • • • • •

WRITE WELL, AND I DON'T MEAN just on the essay. Everybody knows that you have to carefully proof the essays. But you have to write with purpose on the entire application. As applications for limited spots in colleges increase, admissions committees include more variables in their decision making. A sloppy application is not a way to impress the committee. It's just one easy way for them to weed you out early in the process. Read the whole thing front to back and then read it backward. I found two tiny mistakes when I did it backward.

—G.A.
Fredonia, New York
State University of New York, University at Buffalo

OUCH!

Sending bribes doesn't help. I had my mom bake some cookies and I took them to the admissions officer when I had my interview. He was clearly unhappy, but he said he would not hold it against me if I promised not to do anything like that in the future at any other school. He said he often gets home-baked cookies, candies, and nice baskets of food. He said that never once have those things come into play when a decision was made on a student, so it's really a waste of time.

—*Linda Roadarmel*
Parkersburg, West Virginia
West Virginia University

THE WORST PART OF THE WHOLE process for me was writing the essay. It's hard to come up with something you feel would be adequate. A good way to do it, though, is to find an important experience you worked through and talk about its impact on you.

—*Margaret Judin*
Lawrenceville, Georgia
Agnes Scott College

TRY TO FIGURE OUT WHAT you want and go after it as best you can. Admissions officers and guidance counselors are only interested in positive outcomes (less trouble for the guidance office) and high yield (impressive numbers for the college). But this is *your life!* So, if your heart is set on a particular school and everyone tells you you'll never get in, apply anyway. The worst that can happen is that you're rejected and you go somewhere else, which is what would've happened if you'd never applied.

—*Anonymous*
Brooklyn, New York
P *Beloit College*

TWO STRESS REDUCERS

- Start your essays early. Many schools have essays with common themes, such as an influential person or experience in your life. It helps to start working on ideas for these general essays over the summer, before the academic workload begins.

- Ask for recommendations before you actually need them. It helps to give people a little extra time to write about why you're a great applicant.

—*Bethany Black*
Chapel Hill, North Carolina
University of North Carolina

What to put on your résumé: every single leadership/extracurricular activity you've ever done. Make sure to make it all sound very important, if you can. Don't lie, but instead of "wrote and asked questions at poverty discussion," say "codesigner and forum moderator at poverty discussion." And put the dates to anything you can; it makes it sound more legit.

—*David Berngartt*
Chapel Hill, North Carolina
University of North Carolina

My essay was about ice-skating and how it wasn't something that I enjoyed doing competitively but I rediscovered it as something I enjoyed doing just for me. I got the idea by thinking about something that made me really happy, and I wrote about it. I was having trouble thinking of something before that. I found it easy to pick an emotion and write about that.

—*Emma*
Harrington Park, New Jersey
Brown University

YOU SHOULD NOT PUT SOB STORIES in your essays. A lot of people have deceased loved ones; it's not going to make you a special individual to a college admissions officer. Don't worry so much about writing something that is going to reflect your intelligence so much as your personality. I wrote about an improvisational comedy class that I took. I had a friend who wrote an ode to his favorite pair of socks; he's at Brown now.

—*ZACHARY KLION*
SUFFERN, NEW YORK
YALE UNIVERSITY

Keep it short and to the point. You're not writing *War and Peace*. And these people have tons of essays to read.

—*MILLER SMATHERS*
FINDLAY, OHIO

SCHOOLS GET THOUSANDS OF ESSAYS and it's difficult to stand out from the pack. I opened my essay with an anecdote, one that captured my personality and my experience, and I think this caught attention. In my essay, I also stressed unique reasons why I wanted to attend the school I was applying to. I didn't keep it general (saying something such as, "your school has a great history department"); instead, I mentioned professors' names whom I wanted to learn from and why, and I mentioned some of the special qualities that I felt the school had.

—*ANDREA*
TORONTO, ONTARIO
QUEEN'S UNIVERSITY

MY LIFE, THE GAME

Think your application is creative? Claremont McKenna College in California says one applicant sent in a homemade board game based on this applicant's life. Chocolate dice and trivia questions on things like such as the student's pet rat highlighted the game. The student, for all that creativity, was wait-listed.

KEEP ORGANIZED WITH APPLICATION DATES. I almost missed my housing deadline and would've had to go back in line if that happened.

—*LAUREN SHER*
GAINESVILLE, FLORIDA
UNIVERSITY OF FLORIDA

"Use the thumb test. I put my thumb over my name at the top of my essay and ask myself, 'Can anyone else's name go there as the author?' You want your essay to be so unique that you would be the only possible author."

—*KELLY TANABE*
CALIFORNIA
HARVARD UNIVERSITY

MAKE YOURSELF KNOWN: Call the school you are interested in until you can determine who will be reviewing your application. Don't be afraid to leave that person multiple messages until all of your questions are answered. I felt that it was much less likely that they'd eliminate me for asking too many questions as opposed to showing very little interest.

—*G.A.*
FREDONIA, NEW YORK
STATE UNIVERSITY OF NEW YORK, UNIVERSITY AT BUFFALO

DEAR COLUMBIA: I LOVE HARVARD

When you complete and submit essays or letters of recommendation, check to make certain the letters are going to the right schools. In other words, make sure your essay to the University of Nevada doesn't say, "I've always dreamed of attending Arizona State University." I know it sounds like a no-brainer, but it can get hectic when you are sending out so many of these letters. I caught myself with a letter to NYU sealed in an envelope addressed to Buffalo. Luckily, I realized what I was doing before I actually put it in the mailbox. I was imagining myself trying to reach in and get the letter out of there. Getting nailed with a federal offense is not a good idea when you're about to start college.

—*Alan Wolf*
Fredonia, New York
State University of New York, University at Buffalo

I APPLIED TO 16 DIFFERENT SCHOOLS and had to write a variety of essays. I had five different people working with me on my essays, trying to perfect them. This, while balancing the academics of my senior year, proved to be difficult. I lessened the stress by allowing myself time off to play various sports; physical activity has always let me take my mind off work.

—*Andrew Wung*
Diamond Bar, California
University of California, San Diego

YOUR DATA, IN ORDER OF IMPORTANCE

GPA is the first thing schools look at. The second, the strength of your schedule: how rigorous were the courses you took; how hard were you pushing. Tests are usually the third thing schools look at.

In the view of the admissions office, grades and performance in high school are the best indicators of success for your first year of college because they demonstrate what kind of student you are.

MY DAUGHTER'S FRIEND, who is a year older, told her to write about something that others wouldn't be writing about. My daughter wrote an essay about the day she persuaded a couple to adopt a pet at a Humane Society adoption center. She wrote it from a very personal point of view, which really conveyed her passion for animals and for people.

—*ROBERT*
ATLANTA, GEORGIA
UNIVERSITY OF PENNSYLVANIA

I'M TAKING A CREATIVE NONFICTION class right now. Our professor's piece of advice was to think about the thing that really makes you crazy and different from anyone else, something that no one would ever expect. That can be applied to your college admissions essay. Go for the little interesting thing that makes you unique. My essay was about this strange obsession I had with Shakespeare when I was nine years old.

—*CAROLINE*
HAMILTON, MASSACHUSETTS
BROWN UNIVERSITY

I HELPED WITH MY SON'S ESSAYS by talking through the subject with him. I guided him to write about personal experiences and to be creative. For example, one essay he wrote was in the form of an e-mail exchange with his parents.

—*Beth Reingold Gluck*
Atlanta, Georgia
P University of Southern California

"Have a purpose for your essay. Are you telling a story? If so, make sure it is clear. The readers are looking for clarity in your composition, not at your SAT vocabulary."

—*Sarah Bormel*
Baltimore, Maryland
Boston University

I WROTE ONE ESSAY. I wrote it at the last minute and I didn't revise it all. I don't know if that's a good approach. That's my writing style and maybe not for others. Ultimately, they're not going to get a sense of you as a whole person from this one essay. And the throw-it-all-in approach is not as successful because it doesn't sound as true. It sounds as if you're trying to build a résumé rather than tell them who you are. Just focus on one thing that shows who you are.

—*Anastasia*
Baltimore, Maryland
Yale University

PARENT TO PARENT

I hired a woman who helped my son with the application process. I knew it was a lot to deal with, and was aware that kids will generally respond more quickly and thoroughly to someone who is an expert in the field, as opposed to a parent. There are just too many buttons that get pushed with parents and kids. That said, even with my intention to back off and stay relaxed, there were moments when I found myself checking in with him more often than I should have. When he told me he had it covered, I just had to trust that he did, because ultimately he was the one who was going to have to live with the result.

—*Linda Salazar*
Palos Verdes, California
P Brooks Institute of Photography

Be yourself in your essay. That's all I did. My essay was about my worst fear, which at the time was sharks. I had learned to surf, and one day when I was surfing I saw two sharks swimming by me. I lifted my legs and arms out of the water and let them go by me. I wasn't hurt, and I realized I had faced my fear. Since that moment, I haven't been afraid of them. That's what I wrote about in my essay.

—*Jennifer Dragovich*
Seminole, Florida
Florida State University

IT WASN'T SO MUCH WHAT I talked about in my college admissions essay, but *how* I talked about it. I compared my grandmother to clementines (the fruit), and I carried the concept throughout. It was quirky, but I made it work, and that essay made every college I applied to think I was a quirky yet interesting person. More than anything else, it showed that I could communicate well, which is one of those "have it or perish!" skills.

—Erin
Tacoma, Washington

CHOOSE A DAY AND DESIGNATE how much of the application you are going to get done; the next week you can do another part. Write down the essay topics; many schools have the same topics. Brainstorm two to three instances to write about that have occurred in your life, that pertain to the topic. As you do this, you can probably write one essay and change it around to fit each question.

—Tillie
Houston, Texas
Chatham College

DEAR EVERYONE

An estimated 270 colleges accept the Common Application, making it easier for a student to apply to a large number of institutions.

My college essay was about my mom telling me when I was a kid that she was gay. It was about that experience. I come from a really stifled conservative town. The essay was about a lot of conflicting ideas that I saw around me. It showed personal awareness. Write something you're passionate about.

—Chloe
Litchfield, Connecticut
Brown University

"Don't go crazy with the colors. While it stands out less, standard black ink is more legible than hot pink. I wrote my first draft in red, and when my dad saw it he nearly blew a gasket."

—C.D.
New Middletown, Ohio
Youngstown State University

In writing essays, it's best to focus on what makes you unique. Whether it comes out through the subject you choose or your writing style or both, it's your personality that will make your essay grab the attention of admissions people. Don't just try to say what you think they want to hear: No one's going to buy it if you tell them your favorite activity is studying.

—Colin Campbell
Charlottesville, Virginia
University of North Carolina

WHAT *NOT* TO PUT IN YOUR ESSAY

YOUR ABILITY TO DO KEG STANDS: a valuable asset once you reach college, but maybe not what admissions people would like to hear.

—Nathaniel Cohen
West Hartford, Connecticut
New York University

ANYTHING ABOUT BOYFRIENDS or music camp.

—Christiana
New York, New York
Columbia University

YOU SHOULD PROBABLY LEAVE OUT INFORMATION about how many mailboxes you smashed or about the time you puked in the bathroom at the prom.

—Scott Coolbaugh
Knoxville, Tennessee
University of Tennessee

ADMISSIONS OFFICERS AREN'T LIKELY to be impressed that you once took 20 shots of vodka in one sitting.

—Colin Campbell
Charlottesville, Virginia
University of North Carolina

I MADE SURE THAT I had a lot of different people proofread my essays for me, including my parents and teachers. I didn't want to forfeit my chances of getting into a school because I had simple spelling or grammatical errors.

—Carrie Bertolozzi
Chapel Hill, North Carolina
University of North Carolina

• • • • • • • •

I WAS DOING SOMETHING so revolutionary in my family that I was completely stressed over it. I took a lot of long, thoughtful walks my senior year of high school. I also spoke to several of my siblings' friends who were in college.

—Nancy Poehlmann
Atlanta, Georgia
Agnes Scott College

• • • • • • • •

WRITE WITH CONFIDENCE. Don't be cocky, but be straightforward and clear.

—Scott Coolbaugh
Knoxville, Tennessee
University of Tennessee

• • • • • • • •

I DON'T THINK COLLEGES like to read essays that are just an explanation of your activities list. Try to write your essay about a specific quality you possess or a lesson learned. And it always helps to add some humor into your essay. Self-deprecating humor is always very effective in situations like this. I wrote about how I felt that I had the leadership ability to be the captain of the basketball team, but was overlooked. That shows that I feel I am a leader but that I am also big enough to handle defeat well: Kind of kills two birds with one stone.

—Alan Wolf
Fredonia, New York
State University of New York, University at Buffalo

ASK THE EXPERT

What is the school really looking for in an interview?

A school wants to see two things: your character, talent, and interests not shown in the application (or the interests in more detail); and your interest in the school. An interviewer, as an outside third party, "vouches" for you. He observes—and often confirms—what can be read and surmised in other parts of your application. Show that you have something to add to the school. You do not have to be loud to be a leader and contributor, but you need to brag and present yourself. Make sure to convey your research and interest in the school.

WITH THREE COLLEGES and soon to be a fourth under my belt, I have obviously had a lot of college experiences, both good and bad. I have done the whole application process, oh, thousands of times. (Actually, I've submitted something like 15 applications.) This is what I've learned: Be real in your admission essay. You don't want to read a list of achievements in essay form; neither do admissions people. Use humor; it generally goes over well. Set yourself apart from other students: Have you done something others haven't? Are you somewhat different? Write about it! Put your heart and soul into your essay, believe what you are writing, write about something you care about. It'll make the task that much easier.

—*Courtney Heilman*
Boston, Massachusetts

HEADS UP: ON COLLEGE INTERVIEWS

Many colleges and universities offer the opportunity for an interview to try to get to know you beyond the application.

WHAT WILL THEY ASK?

A good interviewer should not try to trap you or test you. The interview is a chance to get to know you. For example, if English is your favorite class and you love to read, you should be asked about your favorite book. You should not be asked about your stance on world politics (unless, of course, you tell the interviewer that you are politically active).

There are a few topics, however, that you should always be prepared to answer at any interview:

1. Why are you interested in the school?

2. What are your plans for academic study? (At many schools, being undecided is fine.)

3. What are the things you bring to the school; what are your passions?

HOW TO MAXIMIZE YOUR INTERVIEW

1. Research the school beforehand. Even just a few minutes surfing their Web site can help. Think about what is actually drawing you to the school.

2. Be yourself. Let the interviewer see what makes you tick. Honest answers about your passions and your personality will help you shine.

3. Engage with the interviewer. Ask what has kept him connected to the school and how the school has affected his life. Ask questions about the school to explore the fit. You have more power in the interview than you think; *they* are trying to sell the school to *you*!

4. Follow up the interview by writing a thank-you note or e-mail. It signifies respect for your interviewer's time and shows your interest.

When you're spending hours on applications and essays, don't forget music; it's a great stress reliever.

—*Briana*
Sonoma, California
Sonoma State University

I wrote my essay on being editor of my yearbook, and my three years involved with it. I think it made a difference, since I could convey a hard-work ethic (staying at school until 3 a.m., taking work home with me), as well as a passion for what I did. It's good to write honestly and candidly about something that has touched you, since it's harder to BS something you feel strongly about; and over-the-top, SAT-word-saturated essays can definitely set off the BS alarm.

—*Tricia Powell*
Huntington Beach, California
University of California, Berkeley

Make sure to use active and not passive verbs. Instead of writing "I was given the award by the local chapter of the NAACP," write "The local chapter of the NAACP awarded me ..." See how much better that sounds?

—*Tabitha Hagar*
Wilmington, Delaware
University of Delaware

The most important aspect of the essay is picking the right subject. And how do you do that? Ask yourself this: What are your major accomplishments, and why do you consider them accomplishments? Don't limit yourself to only accomplishments for which you have been formally recognized. The most interesting essays often are based on accomplishments that may have been trite at the time, but become crucial when placed in the context of your life. I used teaching my little brother to ride his bike as the subject of my essay.

—*K.R.*
Winchester, Virginia
University of Virginia

MAKE THE MOST OF YOUR EXPERIENCES

Almost every school requires an essay—Michigan actually required three—and many of them ask you to write about some obstacle you've overcome. We were a little worried because our daughter really hadn't faced too many obstacles in her life. Not that everything had been easy all the time, but she hadn't been in a hurricane or anything. We decided that in the end, the schools really just wanted to see if you could write. So for one essay, she wrote about the volunteer work that she had done on the Paul Wellstone campaign and how devastating it was when he was killed in the plane crash before the election; and how she had gone on to work on the campaign of Walter Mondale, who ended up losing. On another, she talked about being in Italy as an exchange student in high school and how people there had a really different sense of their body image, being less uptight and letting it all hang out, so to speak, and how she had had to rethink her own feelings about body images. So these weren't really terrible personal obstacles, but they showed that she could think clearly and write a decent essay.

—*M.B.*
MINNEAPOLIS, MINNESOTA
P UNIVERSITY OF MICHIGAN

ESSAY WRITING DON'TS

Don't write what you think a committee wants to hear. The more you try to craft something for them, the more it will fall flat. You never know who will be reading your application or what they are seeking. They just want to know what makes you tick. There are very few topics a reader has not seen, so just be yourself!

Don't write in a style that is not yours. The essay should reflect your personality. It is disappointing to see an essay written in a severe and formal style from someone who is clearly known for a sense of humor. On the flip side, an essay should not be an attempt to entertain the reader, but if you are more casual, you can be a bit relaxed (with proper grammar and language). But please do not attempt humor if you are a serious person; it is simply painful to read.

Don't have someone else write it. A committee knows when something sounds "wrong" in an essay because they read thousands of essays a year. There are also testing data and grades for English in the application, so if the writing is very different from those indicators, a reader will know something is fishy. Do not make this mistake and lose your chance of admission.

Don't vastly exceed page limits or word limits. A well-written essay can say everything you want or need in the limits of the essay. If you cannot seem to write close to those limits, you are likely going off-topic or talking about unnecessary things. An essay should be about a small, focused thing—not a broad discussion—and this should be kept to about a page or two.

Don't play with margins and fonts to squeeze in more. What you are doing is obvious, and if you happen to be the 30th application of the day for the reader and your font is small, it is not fun.

DON'T BE AFRAID TO WRITE about topics that are controversial, because they can make the best essays. When asked to choose a topic on issues that were important to us, I wrote one of my essays on the death penalty. I also wrote one about why I wanted to be a teacher and how I was inspired by my late father's career. I would definitely recommend topics close to your heart, because it's just easier to write when you have a passion for the subject.

—Ellana Mandel
Riverdale, New York
Sarah Lawrence College

GET MULTIPLE PEOPLE TO READ OVER your college essay, especially people who know a lot about it, such as a good guidance counselor. Or take it to a university and say, "Can someone read this? Is it good?" I doubt more than two people read my college essays for me. Looking back, the essay is more important than the tests.

—Ahmad
Basking Ridge, New Jersey
Stanford University

AS SOMEONE WHO APPLIED to only one school, I happen to think it's a phenomenal idea: I wrote only one essay, sent in only one application fee. However, take that with an entire shaker of salt, since I got into the one school to which I applied. Also, I applied early, meaning that while I put a significant share of my eggs in one basket, if I had been rejected, I would have had just enough time to spend every waking hour banging out a few more essays for my backups.

—Nafi Israel
Newton, Massachusetts
Columbia University

APPLICATION EXPANSION

The number of students who applied to 12 or more colleges increased 50 percent between 2001 and 2005.

THE PRINCETON ESSAY QUESTION WAS, "Who would you have as a roommate?" I mentioned Brooke Shields, since she used to go to the school. It was a silly answer, but I had fun with it. I also mentioned that I've seen the movie *Clash of the Titans* 40 times, and how when I'm bored I recast movies in my head (e.g.: "How would Danny DeVito do as Robin Hood?") I explained that this little game in my head is my escape; it is one random thing that gives me pleasure and provides an outlet for my imagination. I'm sure it's what helped me get into Princeton, because there are 8,000 other Brians who applied to the school who also had good grades and played sports in high school.

—*Brian Rosen*
New York, New York
Princeton University

Before I started writing, I would talk through my essay with a friend, a teacher, or parent. If you don't want to share your ideas, speak your essay into a tape recorder.

—*Kelly Tanabe*
California
Harvard University

GET YOUR FRIENDS, family, and whoever is good with words and proofing to *read* what you write. It's even good just to hear people say, "This sounds funny," or "I don't understand what you're saying here." Have someone on the outside proof!

—*Heather*
Austin, Texas
Austin Community College

KNOW WHAT YOU'RE LOOKING for instead of going in blind and thinking, "Oh, that school sounds nice." I applied to a lot of schools I wouldn't have wanted to go to. The counselors at my school tried to make it seem you had to go to a school they thought was good. I was trying to apply to swanky schools even though they didn't offer programs I wanted or were too far away.

—*Ashley Little*
Flossmoor, Illinois
Marquette University

INTERVIEW DON'TS

Don't wear inappropriate clothing, chew gum, or show up late. Your presentation shows that you take the interview seriously.

Don't tell stories about crazy behavior, or swear.

Don't forget to ask questions—interviews are a two-way street and you will not seem "engaged" if you do not ask a few things in return.

Don't worry about being perfect, or about being a perfect package—you do not know what a school or an interviewer wants. Frankly, "perfect" interviews with too-practiced answers are boring and seem fake.

Don't forget that you are only in high school. Relax—you are not expected to have all the answers or to have already solved world problems.

KEEP TRACK OF WHICH FORMS you've sent to which college. My brother turned in all the necessary information, but never followed up to make sure that his schools had actually received it. As it turned out, his SAT scores never arrived at Rice, so he wasn't accepted there. Be sure to double-check that the colleges you're applying to have gotten your complete application.

—*Nicoline Strom-Jensen*
Atlanta, Georgia
Agnes Scott College

COLLEGE INTERVIEW TIPS

BE PREPARED AND READY FOR ANY QUESTION they may ask and think of an answer that is not obvious. Know the history of the school and the basics of the program that you are applying for. Smile.

—*Casey Bond*
Grand Rapids, Michigan
Grand Valley State University

• • • • • • • •

I THINK YOU SHOULD TREAT A COLLEGE INTERVIEW like a job interview: Be polite and professional, dress nicely, and send the interviewer a thank-you note afterwards.

—*Elizabeth Bristol*
North Attleboro, Massachusetts
Mount Holyoke College

• • • • • • • •

IF YOU ARE ON THE CUSP IN TERMS OF QUALIFICATIONS, a personal appointment to speak with an admissions officer can help a lot. Having a face to go with an application makes it harder to turn that application down.

—*Allison Greco*
Yardley, New Jersey

• • • • • • • •

DURING INTERVIEWS WITH COLLEGES, be prepared to answer questions like, "What could you see yourself doing someday?" "Why have you chosen this major?" If you go into the interview with no idea how you will answer the tough questions, you could be in trouble.

—*G.A.*
Fredonia, New York
State University of New York, University at Buffalo

MAKE A POINT OF LEARNING ABOUT that school's values, because you'll impress the interviewer more if it's clear that you cared enough to do your research. Also, if they've given you an idea of what sort of questions you'll be asked, be sure to think about your answers in advance. I waited until I was in the car the morning of my interview before I even thought about what I was going to say, and I had to brainstorm with my mom the whole way.

—EMILY ROSE
ATLANTA, GEORGIA
AGNES SCOTT COLLEGE

AS HORRIBLY CLICHÉD AS IT SOUNDS, you have to be yourself in an interview. It's important to be able to act natural, to admit when you don't know something, and even tell a joke or two. Obviously, you should also remain respectful and intelligent.

—KATIE
NEW YORK, NEW YORK
NEW YORK UNIVERSITY

DO SOME HEAVY READING ON A COUPLE OF NEW, exciting books before you go to the interview and then work them into the conversation. Interviewers are always impressed to know that you are reading and keeping up with what's going on in the world.

—ANONYMOUS
BROWNSVILLE, MARYLAND
UNIVERSITY OF MARYLAND

DON'T USE INAPPROPRIATE E-MAIL addresses when writing to admissions officers. One of my friends used the address mikelikesithot@somethingor other.com. Things like that make a really bad impression.

—ALAN WOLF
FREDONIA, NEW YORK
STATE UNIVERSITY OF NEW YORK, UNIVERSITY AT BUFFALO

"During the interview, smile a lot. When you smile, it shows that your attitude and heart are in the interview; your nerves will also settle down so that you can answer questions clearly."

—MAILE CERIZO
MAUI, HAWAII
POINT LOMA NAZARENE UNIVERSITY

IT TOOK ME ABOUT THREE WEEKS to do the college essay. I had to write about an experience that changed the course of my life. I knew I would write about Lyme disease, which I suffered through, but I kept thinking, "How in the world do you sum up the most difficult years of your life in 500 words?" It just seemed impossible no matter how hard I tried. Then, at about 1 a.m., I sat down with a notebook and a pen, and I wrote the essay in about 30 minutes.

—K.E.
HERNDON, VIRGINIA
GEORGE MASON UNIVERSITY

HEADS UP: THE COMMON APPLICATION

Launched in 1976, the Common Application is offered by a group of more than 275 colleges and universities in the U.S. Using the Common App for admission streamlines the process, since you only have to fill out the form once. In spite of its convenience, the Common App has caused only about a 3 to 4 percent increase in applications overall—not as many as you'd think. Some experts feel that there are bad as well as good aspects of the Common App:

PRO

- takes less time and effort so you can apply to more schools
- you can choose among four essays or write your own
- easier to use than a lot of schools' applications
- if you fill it out online, you can save it at any point and go back to it
- you can cut, paste and move things around

CON

- easier to apply to too many schools
- less opportunity to show specific things about yourself
- not as much depth

ASK THE EXPERT

If you came to the school for an overnight visit and your host hated you or you partied hard...will it get back to the AO?

Rule of thumb: Don't do anything to jeopardize your chances of admission. Your behavior can always get back to an admissions officer. AOs do not require you to be pure and sweet, but give them only reasons to love you. At schools where character is a big part of the admission process, positive stories about you can only help.

STAY ON TASK WITH EVERYTHING. I missed applying to one school because the deadline was in August; I assumed that, because applications to all the other schools I was looking at were due in January or February, this one was, too. But then I looked online and found the application deadline had passed.

—*DANE SKILBRED*
SAINT PAUL, MINNESOTA
SANTA CLARA UNIVERSITY

NO MATTER WHOM YOU ARE DEALING WITH, whether it's a high school teacher or counselor or an admissions person or an interviewer, don't swear and don't show up late for a meeting. I did both of those the very first time I met with one of my high school teachers to ask for a recommendation. He really got on me about it and said if I did those things at the wrong time, it could really affect my future. I really took that advice to heart.

—*RACHEL LYNCH*
FREDERICK, MARYLAND
COPPIN STATE UNIVERSITY

MAKE SURE THE COLLEGES that you apply to know how thoughtful and thorough you were in the process of selecting them. Make them feel special, not as if you just picked them out of the phone book. You can do this by making reference to specific and distinctive characteristics of the college and how those characteristics fit your abilities, personality, and style particularly well. I told schools that I was good at working independently and didn't require much interpersonal interaction with the teachers. I knew this would appeal to bigger schools where many of the freshman classes could number more than 100 students.

—*G.A.*
FREDONIA, NEW YORK
STATE UNIVERSITY OF NEW YORK, UNIVERSITY AT BUFFALO

CHOOSE UNIQUE TOPICS FOR THE ESSAYS. The readers tire of reading the same essays over and over again, so even if your topic is not the most obvious, the reader will appreciate it.

—*CASEY BOND*
GRAND RAPIDS, MICHIGAN
GRAND VALLEY STATE UNIVERSITY

KEEP THE FOCUS ON YOU. Whether you are writing about your favorite book, an influential person, or your favorite subject, remember that your essay needs to convey something about you to the college.

—*KELLY TANABE*
CALIFORNIA
HARVARD UNIVERSITY

WHEN FALL IS HELL

Stressful doesn't begin to describe it! In retrospect, I applied to far too many colleges (nine), so from November to January, I was wrestling with a barrage of applications, essays, recommendations, and test scores. Eventually, I learned to relax and even laugh a little at the whole song-and-dance routine. At my school, when the early-decision letters started arriving, we held a "Wait-Listing Party," complete with cake and "Hello, my name is _______ and I was wait-listed at _______" stickers. It's important to realize that after you send in the application, there's nothing more to be done. Relax!

—*Emily Wachtel*
Agoura Hills, California
University of California, Los Angeles

Proofread, proofread, proofread. And when you are sure it's good, proofread it again. Nothing says, "I did this at the last possible moment" like an "are" instead of "our." And your computer's spell-checker is not going to pick that up for you. Another good thing to do is to read it backwards. That helps. On my last reading I found a "their" that was supposed to be a "there": That was close!

—*Miller Smathers*
Findlay, Ohio

I PORED OVER MY ADMISSIONS ESSAY for Columbia for three months. I wrote, rewrote, edited, proofread, and scoured it for any imperfection. I really tried to give the admissions committee a clear picture of my roots, my ambitions, and my achievements. Clear, effective, and concise prose is the best way to make a statement in your admissions essay. Also, humor is fine if you're a comedian. I am not, so I stuck to a serious tone. Bring your admissions essay to at least one of your high school English teachers to edit—not just for content but also for grammar. Even the smallest typo or grammatical no-no can tarnish an otherwise great personal statement.

—*Daniel*
Wheeling, West Virginia
Columbia University

"Write about something that makes you unique but not weird."

—*Allison Leve*
Baltimore, Maryland
New York University

DON'T BRAG A LOT ON YOUR ESSAY; there's a temptation to show off. One of my essays was about how I failed three driving tests. That shows more about character. It shows you can overcome something.

—*Paul*
Chappaqua, New York
Yale University

I'M TAKING A CLASS NOW and the professor was talking about the definition of literary criticism, the purpose of the field. Her point was that literature is something that can improve the human experience and make better people. That's the best material for a college essay. Your essay and the way you approach college should all move toward this idea that you're going to be a better person through college. You're going to learn from the experience. Put that in a college essay.

—*CHRISTIANA*
NEW YORK, NEW YORK
COLUMBIA UNIVERSITY

Extracurriculars: Activities That Help You Stand Out

"Got sun at the neighborhood pool": an extracurricular activity that won't impress colleges. "Served as a lifeguard at neighborhood pool for three consecutive summers": an extracurricular activity that will *impress colleges. Admissions officers want students who show enthusiasm for activities outside of school and display leadership skills. However, they are trained to spot students who engage in extracurriculars that only serve to pad their résumé. Where do you find the balance? We asked students.*

DO ANYTHING THAT DISPLAYS leadership. Practically every job I've applied for over the summer lists "leadership" as one of the primary characteristics. This doesn't have to be formal leadership, but jobs in which you can display some sort of initiative always help.

—*NAFI ISRAEL*
NEWTON, MASSACHUSETTS
COLUMBIA UNIVERSITY

DO SOMETHING THAT YOU ENJOY; IF YOU ARE HAPPY, YOUR PASSION AND EXCITEMENT WILL BE EVIDENT.

—*NICOLE SPENCE*
WYCKOFF, NEW JERSEY
EMORY UNIVERSITY

- Choose activities you're enthusiastic about.
- Explore your options: classes, volunteering, travel, or summer job.
- Try something new and different to expand your horizons.
- Don't let your demanding activities steal time from your schoolwork.
- Try not to burn yourself out before you even get to college.

ONE WEEK EVERY SUMMER for three years, I went on a church mission trip to the Appalachian Mountains to repair flood-damaged homes. I didn't realize it before I applied, but the parts on UNC's application concerning extracurriculars were based on the activities you spent the most time on. That is, they weren't going to be impressed if you did 10 or 12 things, but only spent a few weeks on them during your entire course of high school. They were looking for activities that continued over the years. That is why I am glad that I completed the service project three summers in a row instead of just doing it once.

—Carrie Bertolozzi
Chapel Hill, North Carolina
University of North Carolina

I WORKED AT A LOCAL RADIO STATION as a newscaster and DJ most of my summers during high school. Given that my academic and professional interest is in journalism and broadcasting, I think this experience looked good to admissions people. Also, it's unique: Working retail or being a camp counselor is all well and good, but lots of people are putting that stuff on their application and it probably won't make you stand out from the others.

—Colin Campbell
Charlottesville, Virginia
University of North Carolina

College admissions officers just want to know that you weren't sitting around all summer with cheese doodle crumbs all over your shirt.

—D.T.
Brunswick, Maryland
American University

AS SOMEONE WHO WORKED in the admissions office as a student, I can say that extracurricular activities play a huge part in acceptance. Obviously, if you are a straight-A student your chances are good, but if you are an average student, extracurriculars help a lot. Showing that you can multitask, take the lead, and be involved means a lot to admissions officers.

—Allison Greco
Yardley, New Jersey

THE SUMMER OF MY FRESHMAN YEAR, I interned at a local law firm. There, I learned the skill set it takes to be a successful attorney. Besides that, I worked a job in retail and enjoyed my free time. My summer had a perfect balance: It kept me busy, but left me in a low-stress environment. I would recommend any possible internship that piques your interest. It is important to keep an active lifestyle, as you don't want to be cooped up at home all summer watching reruns of *All in the Family*.

—Scott G.
Chesterfield, Missouri
University of Illinois

I BUILT MY OWN WEB SITE about my life; it was so easy. I think admissions officers like to check out sites like that. It shows them that you are willing to try new things.

—*Linda Roadarmel*
Parkersburg, West Virginia
West Virginia University

"I became involved in one club at my school, the National Forensics League. I decided to pick one club that mattered to me, and to stick with it."

—*Kristina*
Raleigh, North Carolina
University of North Carolina at Greensboro

I DID A LOT OF TRAVELING during the summer. I went on a tour to Israel with the Birthright Oranim program. It was amazing; I ended up staying for 10 days in Israel, touring and visiting family, and loved it. It was my first time on a plane by myself and I think that was good prep for college. After the Israel trip, I went with my family to Costa Rica for a week. I had the time of my life last summer and I think my experience gave me a lot more independence. I can now do laundry. Who would've thought?

—*Barak Krengel*
Dallas, Texas
University of Kansas

A YEAR OFF? PRO AND CON

IT'S FINE TO HAVE A YEAR OFF BETWEEN GRADUATING high school and starting college. I've had college admissions people confirm that to me. But you have to be able to account for that year. To admissions people, it's like a gap on your résumé. It's OK as long as you can explain it away. Don't just say, "I needed some time off," or "I wanted to hang out with my friends for a while." I was able to show them that I used that year to take some classes at a junior college and, in effect, better myself. And I think it helped me emotionally. I'm not sure I would have done as well if I had gone to a four-year school right out of high school. Some people need a little extra prep time. Just make sure you don't waste it.

—Dan Montoya
Youngstown, Ohio
Ohio State University

• • • • • • • •

DON'T TAKE A YEAR OFF BEFORE COLLEGE. I know it's tempting, but don't do it. It's going to come down to you explaining what you did with this lost year, and there's no way to put a positive spin on mooching off your parents for a year while you spent most nights drinking with your friends. You'll have plenty of time for that after you put in your eight years of college to get a four-year degree.

—D.T.
Brunswick, Maryland
American University

• • • • • • • •

I TOOK A YEAR OFF BEFORE COLLEGE TO HAVE SOME FUN. It's good to get to know your hometown. If you didn't have that much time in high school, it can be nice to give yourself the summer or spring to do all the things you've wanted to do. I went to a bunch of museums and investigated neighborhoods and did weekend jaunts to different places. That gave me an appreciation for what I was leaving, and it gave me something to come back to.

—Anastasia
Baltimore, Maryland
Yale University

I USED TO BE AFRAID OF FLYING when I was 13, but I got over it. I noticed on the Web how there was no community for fearful flyers. I wanted to take advantage of that and so I started a Web site. Colleges like to see that sort of thing. It wasn't only the fact that I had a Web site; it was that I had a fear, overcame it, and tried to help other people, as well as make a business out of it.

—Dov Kaufmann
Ra'anana, Israel
Princeton University

Don't overextend yourself. It's more impressive to be editor-in-chief of your school newspaper and a junior varsity track runner than a member of 15 varied clubs.

—Tricia Powell
Huntington Beach
University of California, Berkeley

SINCE I WANTED TO MAJOR IN DANCE IN COLLEGE, I attended summer dance programs just about every summer in high school. Auditioning for summer programs really helped me prepare for auditions for colleges. Noting what you've performed on résumés, and what choreographers you've worked with, is also very important.

—Jennifer Keys
Baltimore, Maryland
New York University

I WAS REALLY INVOLVED in my high school's speech and debate team and spent a great deal of my summer reading, and preparing for fall competition. I also had the opportunity to travel with my family to all sorts of exotic locations, including Thailand, China, and, most notably Singapore. I was able to see the world before I needed to buckle down and work, and it was nice to have those opportunities early. In addition, I worked retail during the summer and helped coordinate and coach a summer enrichment camp for middle school students looking to improve their public-speaking skills.

—Coral A. Schneider
Cherry Hills Village, Colorado
University of Southern California

OTHER SIDE OF THE DESK: UNDERSTANDING "YIELD"

Yield: The percentage of accepted students who say "yes" to a college's offer of admission. Colleges want the highest yield they can achieve every year because it raises their perceived prestige or popularity, and changes the way they admit students (high yield equates with a lower number of applicants admitted). Students who carelessly apply with sloppy applications to yield-sensitive schools will likely not be admitted.

GET INVOLVED BECAUSE you *want* to get involved, not because you think that is the key to getting into college. You will excel most in the activities that you enjoy the most. It is in these activities that you will be most likely to assume leadership positions and make the greatest contributions. And this is what colleges are looking for when they analyze your activities.

—*C.D.*
NEW MIDDLETOWN, OHIO
YOUNGSTOWN STATE UNIVERSITY

SEARCH FOR VOLUNTEER OPPORTUNITIES outside your school. Something that has your school's name attached to it makes it seem as if you didn't work very hard to set this up yourself. If you go out there and say, "I'm a high school student, I'm underage, I can't drive, but I do want to help out your organization in some way," you will stand out.

—*CONOR KENNEDY*
WHITESTONE, NEW YORK
BROWN UNIVERSITY

HEADS UP: SUMMER ACTIVITIES

Contrary to popular belief, there is no "right" summer activity that admissions officers want to see. You should have two main choices:

If you need to earn money, find a summer job. Scooping ice cream is just as valid an activity as any if you need to earn money. If you need to take care of siblings or baby-sit, you should feel confident that these are important and valued. Do not feel the pressure to do something "meaningful" if there are other more pressing priorities.

Follow your interests and explore. This can mean taking that summer class in psychology that your high school does not offer, or travel or summer camp. You should pick activities you love and pursue them to their maximum. Do not waste your time on something merely "résumé building." You will not be judged by your activities, only by a lack of activities. Fill in that space of summer activities with something every year, but do make sure you are also taking a small break; admissions officers do want you to have a break!

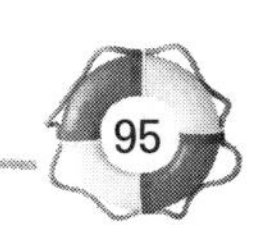

IT'S PRETTY OBVIOUS TO COLLEGES when you're just filling up your résumé. There's no point in doing something you're not excited about just to put it on a résumé, because colleges can see through that anyway. I did a summer sailing program with kids who were released from drug treatment centers or going through drug rehab programs.

—*Anastasia*
Baltimore, Maryland
Yale University

• • • • • • • •

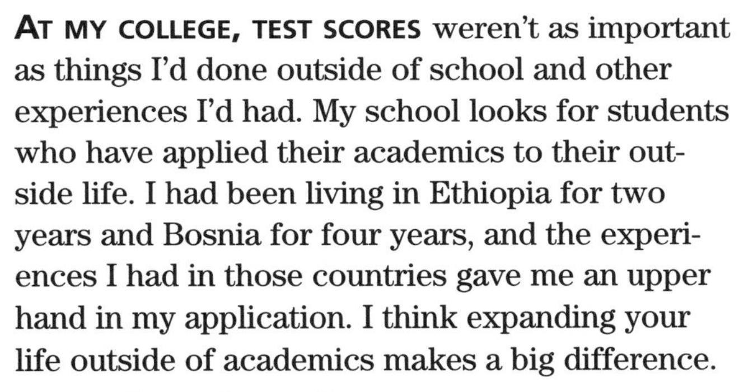

AT MY COLLEGE, TEST SCORES weren't as important as things I'd done outside of school and other experiences I'd had. My school looks for students who have applied their academics to their outside life. I had been living in Ethiopia for two years and Bosnia for four years, and the experiences I had in those countries gave me an upper hand in my application. I think expanding your life outside of academics makes a big difference.

—*Dahvid Castillo-Reminick*
Bronxvile, Florida
Sarah Lawrence College

• • • • • • • •

BE SOCIALLY ACTIVE IN HIGH SCHOOL. Join clubs, sports, and as many organizations as you can. Once you're involved in lots of activities, you can highlight them in your application and show how diverse you are. You've got to stand out. I played soccer and lacrosse in high school; both these activities show team spirit. I was also a member of the National Honor Society. I tutored and was a mentor to younger classmates. I joined the Asian club, and this showed I was in touch with my roots.

—*Kalpana*
Old Bridge, New Jersey
Rutgers University

MY EXTRACURRICULAR ACTIVITIES were possibly the strongest part of my résumé. My summer has always consisted of a day camp where I am a counselor. It's fun, and it pays surprisingly well. Also, I participated in all kinds of clubs in high school and held lots of leadership roles. I served three different leadership positions in the Raleigh Youth Council, including president my senior year. I suggest students join service organizations such as Key Club, and then remember to individually list all the events that you participated in, because it really helps bolster your résumé.

—David Berngartt
Chapel Hill, North Carolina
University of North Carolina

"I did volunteer work for the local athletic association, helping youngsters grow and learn about teamwork. Well, that's what I wrote on the application. All that meant was that I umpired some Little League games. Wording on the application is important, too."

—D.T.
Brunswick, Maryland
American University

ASK THE EXPERT

Does everyone have to be a leader?

What is so important about being a leader? And what, exactly, is leadership? AOs have no written definition of leadership, but they look for students with passion and an outside recognition of this passion. To be a leader, you might be the director of the play or the team captain, but you might also be the quiet, effective stage manager or the unspoken heart of a team. Starting and following a personal project, especially if it is school or community-wide, is leadership. The point is that schools want students who will engage in and make a contribution to the academic and social life of the school, besides partying.

DURING THE SUMMERS I always worked as a tennis counselor for my country club, teaching little kids how to play tennis. It also gave me a greater sense of responsibility and patience.

—*ERICA ROGGEN*
SYRACUSE, NEW YORK
SYRACUSE UNIVERSITY

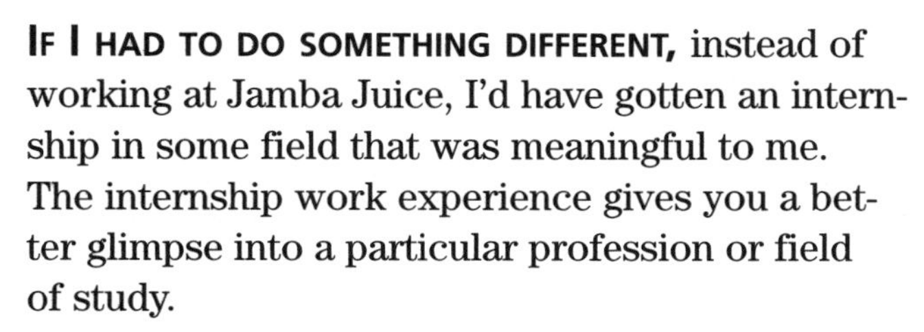

IF I HAD TO DO SOMETHING DIFFERENT, instead of working at Jamba Juice, I'd have gotten an internship in some field that was meaningful to me. The internship work experience gives you a better glimpse into a particular profession or field of study.

—*DAVID LICHTENSTEIN*
SAN DIEGO, CALIFORNIA
UNIVERSITY OF SOUTHERN CALIFORNIA

YOU SHOULD ENJOY WHAT YOU DO in the summer. Don't do something just because you think colleges will like it. I was very involved in my summer camp; every summer of high school I went there for a month. One summer I participated in a University of Maryland one-week science program that I enjoyed.

—*Allison Leve*
Baltimore, Maryland
New York University

THE VOLUNTEER GENERATION

More than 82 percent of high school seniors performed volunteer work in 2004, up from 74 percent a decade earlier and 66 percent in 1989.

EVERYONE WILL TELL YOU IT'S IMPORTANT to be well rounded. I had a really impressive résumé: I was president of my high school, spent a semester abroad during my sophomore year, was an AIDS peer educator, volunteered at a summer camp in Hungary. Be involved in the things you enjoy, but don't leave your grades and board scores behind.

—*Elana Brownstein*
Baltimore, Maryland
University of Maryland, College Park

ONE SUMMER ACTIVITY THAT I participated in was Presidential Classroom, a weeklong program in Washington, D.C., focusing on various issues in politics today. We had seminars, met with representatives of our Congressional offices, visited the State Department and the Saudi Arabian embassy, and celebrated the Fourth of July on the Mall. Colleges love to see that you've challenged yourself during the summer months. It's important to show your desire to continue learning throughout the year, especially outside of the classroom.

—*Bethany Black*
Chapel Hill, North Carolina
University of North Carolina

SUMMER IS THE BEST TIME TO BECOME involved in activities that could combine your recreational interests with productive work. I was fortunate to find a perfect combination to focus on two of my passions. I began as a camper at a theater arts camp and attended it for several years. Then I became an intern and continued to work there for six years. My involvement with one special group showed both my interest in children and the arts. The long history hopefully reflected my commitment.

—*Ellana Mandel*
Riverdale, New York
Sarah Lawrence College

“Do community service. There is something even more rewarding about working for free that you will never experience unless you do it.”

—*Josiah White*
Carrollton, Texas
Oklahoma Baptist University

DURING HIGH SCHOOL SUMMERS, I volunteered in a library and a hospital. Volunteering is a huge part of boosting your résumé for college. I think schools really like people who are ambitious and involved and do things. It shows you have character and that you'll bring that to the school.

—*Mary Kate Taulane*
Huntingdon Valley, Pennsylvania
Loyola College

IF YOU LIVE NEAR A COLLEGE, get a job on campus. The pay is comparable to a lot of part-time jobs, they are extremely flexible, and not all that difficult. You can also make very valuable contacts with administrators and higher-up people in the campus community.

—*ALLISON GRECO*
YARDLEY, NEW JERSEY

ADMISSION OFFICES LIKE TO SEE LEADERSHIP, participation length, and a variety of activities. So while in high school, I was involved in the newspaper for two years: one year as a writer and one year as a features editor. This position thoroughly helped me because I studied journalism, and obviously this looked good. In addition to that, I was on the volleyball team for four years. I served as a Junior and Senior Leader, which meant I assisted a gym teacher with classes and helped with motivation and organization within the class. I assisted with student government events and volunteered often.

—*ANGELA MASSINI*
CHICAGO, ILLINOIS
BUTLER UNIVERSITY

I KNOW WHAT YOU DID LAST SUMMER

Not sure how to describe your summer experience on a college application? Heed the three golden rules:

1. **Keep it real and focus on what your summer actually meant to you.**
2. **Avoid talking about how privileged you were to have had the opportunity to do what you did.**
3. **Find a way to relate your experiences over the summer to your day-to-day life.**

DURING MY SUMMERS, I was able to fit in all the seminars of Dale Carnegie Training (which is basically people-skills training), attend the National Student Leadership Conference in Washington, D.C., volunteer at a Chinese day-care/school, and have a job.

—*Andrew Wung*
Diamond Bar, California
University of California, San Diego

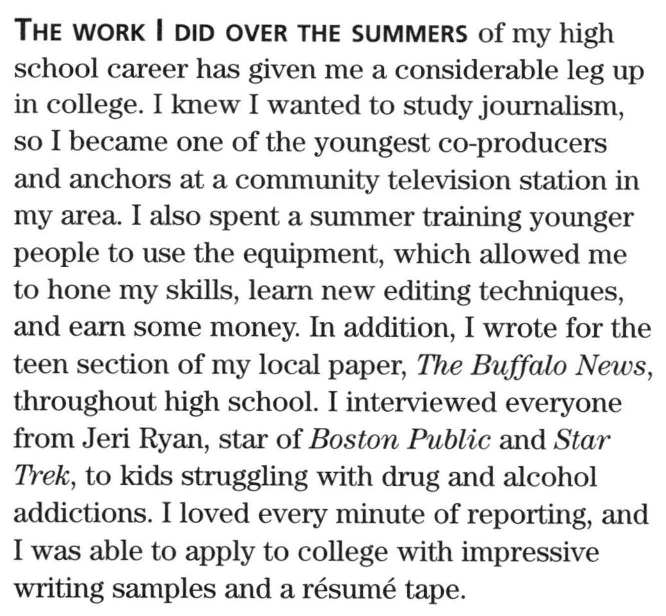

THE WORK I DID OVER THE SUMMERS of my high school career has given me a considerable leg up in college. I knew I wanted to study journalism, so I became one of the youngest co-producers and anchors at a community television station in my area. I also spent a summer training younger people to use the equipment, which allowed me to hone my skills, learn new editing techniques, and earn some money. In addition, I wrote for the teen section of my local paper, *The Buffalo News*, throughout high school. I interviewed everyone from Jeri Ryan, star of *Boston Public* and *Star Trek*, to kids struggling with drug and alcohol addictions. I loved every minute of reporting, and I was able to apply to college with impressive writing samples and a résumé tape.

—*Jason Torreano*
Lockport, New York
State University of New York, Brockport

MY ACTIVITIES WERE MOSTLY SCHOOL CLUBS for art, math, foreign language, Honor Society, things like that. While they were great, I wish I had done more community service, because the scholarships I applied for had a heavy emphasis on community service and philanthropy.

—*David*
Muncie, Indiana
Anderson University

I FOCUSED ON THINGS I was passionate about. For example, I swam when I was growing up and through middle school, so during a few high school summers I taught swimming lessons in addition to lifeguarding. I have also always had a passion for writing, so another summer I attended a creative writing workshop for two weeks through Duke University. Find what you're interested in, be ambitious in pursuing it, and your résumé will build itself.

—*WHITNEY TRITT*
ATLANTA, GEORGIA
WAKE FOREST UNIVERSITY

Being the president of this or that organization looks great on your application. But if you're not the type of person who's interested in that sort of thing, then what's the use?

—*APRIL*
CHICAGO, ILLINOIS
PURDUE UNIVERSITY

ANY EDGE IS GOOD NOWADAYS, but don't make yourself miserable. I took time off during my summers, and I don't regret it. I just loaded up on my college résumé activities during the year. Do what feels right during your summers.

—*MARTIN*
GARDEN GROVE, CALIFORNIA
UNIVERSITY OF CALIFORNIA, LOS ANGELES

OVER THE COURSE OF FOUR SUMMERS, I went to an engineering camp and played in the pit orchestra for three musicals with a local theater group, in addition to summer school and holding a job. I always felt guilty about not doing more, but when I started filling out applications, I realized that there wasn't even enough space to put down everything I did do. Of course, summer activities do leave an impression on the application readers, but not every waking moment of every summer needs to be college focused. Given the chance, I would go back and choose just a few activities that really sparked my interest.

—*EMILY WACHTEL*
AGOURA HILLS, CALIFORNIA
UNIVERSITY OF CALIFORNIA, LOS ANGELES

SUMMER COLLEGE CLASSES

If you are interested in exploring a subject further to broaden your experiences, either at a local college or at one in another city, go for it. However, know that a summer course or other academic experience that requires a fee to participate is not valued any higher than other activities. Choose something for the experience and for your passion, not for your résumé.

SHOW THEM THAT YOU ARE MOTIVATED. Get out and do something worthwhile. And if you can help someone in the process, man, they eat that stuff up.

—*D.T.*
BRUNSWICK, MARYLAND
AMERICAN UNIVERSITY

I WORKED AT AN ELEMENTARY school summer program for four years well before I was concerned with college résumés. I did it because I enjoyed it. I also took a class at the Academy of Art University in San Francisco and had an internship in video editing. I thought at that time that I wanted to go to film school, so I wanted to start learning. I also had a part-time job in an architecture firm and with an interior designer. My family was in both of those fields, so it was easy for me to get little jobs. A genuine interest in learning and the confidence to try new activities is appealing to most universities.

—*KATHERINE SINNOTT*
MENLO PARK, CALIFORNIA
UNIVERSITY OF CALIFORNIA, BERKELEY

ADMISSIONS OFFICERS have really good BS detectors. They know a lot of kids do lots of extracurricular activities just to get in. Look for avenues in which you have a passion. Follow your real interests, as opposed to embellishing your application with a lot of random activities. Even if you don't know, ultimately, what you want to be, your choice of activities should be passion-driven.

—*Tai Milder*
Ukiah, California
University of California, Berkeley

It's important for college admissions officers to see that you have a life outside of school and playing Xbox (unless, of course, you play on the school Xbox team).

— *Ray*
Baltimore, Maryland
Salisbury University

I SIGNED UP FOR EVERY CLUB so I could put them on my applications. If you do that, you also get in all the pictures of the clubs in the yearbook. It's pretty cool. (If I had it to do over again, I would also have been a male cheerleader!)

—*Mitch Royer*
Winamac, Indiana
Indiana University

I HADN'T REALLY CONSIDERED the idea of community service so broadly before. I had wrapped presents, cut turkeys, and done other obvious community work, but as I began to look deeper, I realized I'd spent countless hours at horse-riding competitions, grooming, scoring, and doing errands. I was really surprised at how active I had been in my community over the years, and I was beginning to look a lot more interesting on paper. A lot of my peers, for the purpose of college applications, had been counting their "community hours," and it took me a little while to realize that while they were clocking hours, I was doing things, too, just things specific to me.

—*Heather Muntzer*
Santa Rosa, California
California College of the Arts

Love at First Sight? Visiting Schools

Visits to college campuses are a great way to get a feel for the life you might be living over the next four years. They are also a great way to cut colleges off your list: Many students have taken one look at a campus they thought they would like and decided they would never set foot there again. Others have visited a campus that was low on their list, and they never wanted to leave. What are the most important questions to ask during a visit? How do you get the inside story from students? Before you visit your favorite colleges, visit the following stories and advice.

KEEP AN OPEN MIND: There are many comparable schools and you shouldn't decide you would only be happy by going to one of them. I intentionally did not visit any of the campuses before I found out whether or not I was accepted to the school.

—*ALLISON LEVE*
BALTIMORE, MARYLAND
NEW YORK UNIVERSITY

FIND A RANDOM PERSON TO TALK TO: STUDENTS ARE BRUTALLY HONEST.

—*SARAH BORMEL*
BALTIMORE, MARYLAND
BOSTON UNIVERSITY

- Ask any questions you want; you'll be investing four years and thousands of dollars.
- Timing is important; try to go when students are around and the weather's nice.
- You will do best where you thrive; decide if you can thrive there.
- Jot down your impressions so you'll remember how you felt; it's also material for your essay or interview.
- Politeness counts; always follow up with a thank-you note.

NEVER VISIT ON A WEEKEND MORNING. Several of the colleges were dead when I visited. No one was on campus and there didn't seem to be any atmosphere. Then it hit me: Everyone was still asleep. Now that I am in college, I completely understand why everyone is sleeping. The most important time to visit is later in the afternoon on a spring day. There are more people on campus and I could get a feel for what the school was really like. Spring is amazing: people lying in the quad getting sun, everyone is happy. That is the best time to visit.

—ROB FEHN
BASKING RIDGE, NEW JERSEY
LAFAYETTE COLLEGE

TRUST YOUR FIRST IMPRESSIONS. When I visited Michigan, I didn't really like it. But I went there anyway and was miserable. I went to high school at a small private school and I wasn't into the whole party scene at Michigan. And the academics weren't what I wanted. I left for Brown.

—*ANNE*
PITTSBURGH, PENNSYLVANIA
BROWN UNIVERSITY

"My parents took me on college tours, though on several occasions they dragged me on tours of schools I had no interest in. You, not your parents, should pick your tour itinerary."

—*COLIN CAMPBELL*
CHARLOTTESVILLE, VIRGINIA
UNIVERSITY OF NORTH CAROLINA

A BAD VISITING EXPERIENCE doesn't mean you won't be happy at the school. You might have a bad tour guide or host, or the weather might be gross, making the campus look uglier than you had imagined it. So if you're not sure, visit again; it's worth a second trip to make sure you'll spend the next four years in a place where you feel comfortable.

—*ELANA BROWNSTEIN*
BALTIMORE, MARYLAND
UNIVERSITY OF MARYLAND, COLLEGE PARK

I VISITED THE CAMPUS WITH MY DAD during the summer. It was early in the morning and there were no students on campus. I did not get a feeling for the actual atmosphere. I do remember my dad commenting on how nice the flowers on campus looked, way nicer than they did when he was here 30 years ago.

—*ALLISON RINEY*
YARDLEY, PENNSYLVANIA
UNIVERSITY OF OKLAHOMA

Make sure that there are enough faculty and courses to satisfy your needs.

—*MICHELLE SCHUSTER*
BALTIMORE, MARYLAND
STERN COLLEGE

I VISITED SEVERAL SCHOOLS and I liked the fact that the University of Cincinnati was an urban school with a lot to offer around campus. Later, I gave campus tours, and I was told that most students decide within their first 20 minutes of being on campus whether they want to consider that school or not.

—*ANDREW J. BURKE*
CINCINNATI, OHIO
UNIVERSITY OF CINCINNATI

HAVE CONTACT WITH ACTUAL STUDENTS; you'll get a better sense of things. When I visited Duke, a student yelled out from a window to our tour group, 'Forty-thousand dollars down the drain, man!' Clearly, not everyone there thinks a Duke education is a good value.

—*COLIN CAMPBELL*
CHARLOTTESVILLE, VIRGINIA
UNIVERSITY OF NORTH CAROLINA

LOOK FOR THE BUILDINGS where you will have a lot of classes and notice any landmarks around campus. Landmarks can help you find your way if you get lost.

—*ANGELA FRIEDMAN*
PEORIA, ILLINOIS
BRADLEY UNIVERSITY

RIVALRY 101

I toured UNC on a Friday afternoon in February. It was gorgeous outside, and I remember thinking that the weather was never like this at home in upstate New York. My most vivid memory from the tour came when our guide was discussing the Robertson bus, which runs continuously between UNC and Duke. "It's really great, especially if you have friends at Duke," she said. Without missing a beat, a woman in the back of the tour called out, "Why on earth would we have friends at Duke?" I got my introduction to the Duke-Carolina rivalry right then and there. When you're taking a tour, try to envision yourself living there, studying there, sitting on the quad. If it's hard to picture yourself there, it might not be the place for you. Most importantly, no one can make this decision for you. Just because your grandfather's best friend's nephew went there and loved it doesn't mean that you will.

—Bethany Black
Chapel Hill, North Carolina
University of North Carolina

It's important to realize that a formal tour is formal. They're taking you to see buildings and see what the school physically looks like. To get a real feel for the school, you have to walk around and hang out with people. It's very easy to get in touch with students who are at the school. You can go through the school admissions office, and students are very happy to talk about the school. Ask students questions. The first question I ask is, "Are you happy with the school? Why or why not?" Every student has an opinion.

—Dana
Lawrence, New York
Harvard University

PARENT TO PARENT

An admissions counselor told us, "Watch and listen to your child's initial reaction when they first arrive for their visit." Based on this counselor's experience, your children will know if they are comfortable in this setting within the first 10 minutes on campus. Listen to your kids! Their gut reaction is usually right on.

—*Debbie*
Pittsburgh, Pennsylvania
P Ohio University

I did campus overnights at the colleges I was looking at. These were great experiences and really helped in the decision-making process for college. Great things to look for when on those visits are: campus security, what the dorms are like, the quality of the food served on campus, entertainment for the campus community, facilities. Try to find out what the personality of the student body is at that school.

—*Kelly Parmet*
Houston, Texas
Southwestern University

• • • • • • • •

Look at the quality of the dorm rooms, the measures that the campus has taken for security (do they have emergency call buttons?). Get to know the town (walk around a couple times to get a feel of where you'll be living), visit the registrar's office to get information for the upcoming year, visit the religious center that you may want to become involved in, and find out the type of food they serve (because some places can have a really gross food service).

—*Jenna Iszauk*
Monroeville, Pennsylvania
Ohio University

I KNEW A FRIEND ON THE TULANE CAMPUS and went to visit him. This visit definitely influenced me when I was applying to schools. I fell in love with the city and the campus, and even though my friend wasn't a deciding factor, knowing he was there was a plus.

—*JAMES AROGETI*
ATLANTA, GEORGIA
TULANE UNIVERSITY

"Visit your number one choice last. That way you can compare it to the others with an open mind. If you go to your number one choice first, your opinion of the others will be tainted because you think you have seen what you want."

—*BETSY LILIENTHAL*
WILMINGTON, DELAWARE
UNIVERSITY OF DELAWARE

I DIDN'T VISIT THE CAMPUS before I got to the University of Arizona. I had a friend here who said it was a great school, and I always trusted his opinion. I liked the weather in Tucson and it's not too far from my home in California, but still far enough that I could do my own thing.

—*MICHAEL ABRAMOVITZ*
TUCSON, ARIZONA
UNIVERSITY OF ARIZONA

FROM A TOUR GUIDE'S MOUTH

I'm a campus tour guide at my school, so I know that most of the information we give you is important. You should not focus so much on which buildings you will see, but on what the tour guide is saying as you go through them. Focus on which residence halls you would like to live in and take the suggestions that the tour guides give you. If they recommend a certain hall, they are not only giving you advice from a university standpoint, but also from personal experience. Take notes and pictures during your visit. And, most important, ask questions.

—*David Danenberg*
Kent, Ohio
Kent State University

Convince your parents that you want to get a feel for college life by visiting campuses that some of your friends go to, without your parents coming along. Look up a couple of old friends through Facebook.com or MySpace.com, take some road trips, and see what college is really like when you're not walking around with a tour group and your parents. You're not going to choose a particular college because your father pointed out on the tour that they had the largest research library in the region. The quality of life on campus is a big part and there is no way to know whether you want to go urban or rural, or big or small, unless you actually go and see what it is like to live there.

—*Dominic Berardi*
Cincinnati, Ohio
University of Cincinnati

WHEN YOU VISIT CAMPUSES, find out what the social scene is like. It could make or break your experience. It's a really important outlet, especially if you're going to an educationally rigorous university. And ask about diversity. Find a place that's more diverse than your high school; it makes it fun to learn about other people.

—AHMAD
BASKING RIDGE, NEW JERSEY
STANFORD UNIVERSITY

ASK STUDENTS ABOUT THE RELATIONSHIP they have with their professors. How many professors do they have that relationship with? Are professors accessible? Can you talk to them on a regular basis? That is something that is lacking here. I've had a hard time having one-on-one talks with my professors.

—EMMA
HARRINGTON PARK, NEW JERSEY
BROWN UNIVERSITY

SOME SCHOOLS OFFER AN OVERNIGHT PROGRAM in which you can be housed with a current freshman and be taken to their classes, experience their activities, and just get to know them. Take advantage of this! Visiting Emory opened my eyes to the multiple opportunities available at this university. I was able to see what the other students were like, sat in on classes (getting a decent feel of the structure, professors, other students' work ethic), talked to current undergrads, and just got a general feel of the school. Because of the opportunities, the happiness of the students, and the proximity to the city, my decision was sealed.

—NICOLE SPENCE
WYCKOFF, NEW JERSEY
EMORY UNIVERSITY

Bring your parents, if you can. They'll feel better and be more understanding later when you're at school.

—LAUREN SHER
GAINESVILLE, FLORIDA
UNIVERSITY OF FLORIDA

YAH, MON

Are you ready to laugh? I had visited several schools around Ohio and California trying to decide where I needed to be. I decided upon Bowling Green State University because of two things: One, there was a man standing in the middle of the green in front of our student union selling tie-dyed T-shirts and other hippie-esque garments; Two, it was Bob Marley Week on campus.

It ended up being a great decision because I switched my major to journalism my junior year. BGSU's journalism program is nationally known.

—Hillary
Breckenridge, Colorado
Bowling Green State University

When I visited the school I ultimately chose, I knew I wanted to go there. It was the most miserable day ever. There was black ice on the sidewalk, and my eyelashes were freezing together. And I still wanted to go there, so I figured, "This must be the place." It was a small campus. They had small classes. Everyone was really friendly, I just felt really comfortable there.

—Julie Collins
Des Moines, Iowa
Drake University

Start by looking at the area, not just the college. Don't blow off the college tours, either. Go spend time and money visiting. It's worth your peace of mind.

—Debbie
Homewood, Illinois
P

DON'T LOOK AT SCHOOLS that everyone knows and talks about. You need to find a college that is good for you. When I decided to look at Muhlenberg College, most of my friends said, "Muhlen*what*?" Ignoring their naïveté was the best decision I have ever made. When I visited Muhlenberg I felt right at home. There is no better description than to say that it just felt right. There is no such thing as a "good college." Good is something that one needs to decide for oneself. I suggest having an open mind and not deciding anything about a school until you see it with your own eyes.

—MELISSA BERMAN
MANALAPAN, NEW JERSEY
MUHLENBERG COLLEGE

WHEN I WAS APPLYING, I'd always ask questions about the kind of food that the college served. I knew if they talked about fast food places nearby or dorms that had kitchens, the food must be bad.

—ELIZABETH MILLER
DECATUR, GEORGIA
AGNES SCOTT COLLEGE

IF YOU PLAN TO PARTICIPATE IN AN ACTIVITY, such as the newspaper or the radio station, during your visit speak to students who take part. It's a good way to find out what the people are like and what your chances are of getting involved. I was planning on studying journalism, so going to the student newspaper was one of the first stops I made during my first visit to campus. The students were very supportive and told me to go for it. It puts your mind at ease once you've made the initial contact with those groups.

—BRIAN SNIDER
YOUNGSTOWN, OHIO
YOUNGSTOWN STATE UNIVERSITY

Visit the school during a tour. Walk around campus with your family; see if you feel the right vibe.

—LAUREN MARCINIAK
BURR RIDGE, ILLINOIS
BRADLEY UNIVERSITY

VISIT SCHOOLS BEFORE YOU COMMIT. I was almost 100 percent certain that I was going to MIT. Then I got the acceptance letter from Stanford and became mildly interested. By pure chance, I was out in California for a baseball tournament and I took a day off and visited the university. I figured I might as well see it, even though I probably wouldn't go. It was a beautiful day on campus. It's like a country club. I called my dad and said, "Dad, I think I'm going to Stanford." If I hadn't visited, I really think I would not have gone there.

—*AHMAD*
BASKING RIDGE, NEW JERSEY
STANFORD UNIVERSITY

"I was very direct while talking to people about the school. It's OK to be critical; you are investing four years and thousands of dollars. It's a big deal. Don't be afraid to ask what you want to know. You aren't being rude; you are being smart and proactive."

—*ZACH HANDLER*
ST. LOUIS, MISSOURI
BRANDEIS UNIVERSITY

LETTER FROM A HAPPY PARENT

We started by looking around at colleges when we were vacationing, but our son Ben really wasn't ready. The summer between his sophomore and junior year, for example, we were out west in San Francisco and looked at Berkeley and Stanford and a couple of others, but he just wasn't clicking with them. The following summer I had a trip to D.C. and we showed him George Washington University and Georgetown; he didn't really like either one.

As the time got closer, he and my husband, Tom, did this emergency trip: Tom had a conference in New York City and Ben went with him and spent time checking out NYU and Columbia and he was just totally overwhelmed—it was too much stimuli—so they decided to just get in the car and start driving. They saw about 10 schools and jumped into whatever tours they could catch along the way. At one Ivy League school, it happened to be Parents Day, and they were turned off by all the wealth and expensive cars.

When they got to Skidmore, things went really well: They had a good tour person and the theater was open for Ben to see. When they got back, Ben did further investigation and narrowed his choices to seven schools. He got into Skidmore and has been happy there so far.

As parents, we're very pleased with the way things turned out. Skidmore is a little cocoon, and he's really thriving on the smaller classes and individual attention from professors. We're so glad it worked out for him.

—*Victoria Johnson*
Minneapolis, Minnesota
P Skidmore College

HEADS UP: ON IVIES

Although the term Ivy League was originally coined to refer to a collegiate athletic conference, the eight Ivy League universities that form the group are certainly among the best in the world. All the Ivies are old—most were founded during the colonial period—private Northeastern institutions. All were founded as men's colleges but have accepted women since the 1970s. Here are some things to consider about the Ivy League:

- In today's highly competitive world of admissions, Ivies have among the lowest rates of acceptance. There is not nearly enough room for all the students who are qualified.
- Each Ivy is unique, not only in size and atmosphere, but also as a result of location. You will have a different experience at Columbia University in urban New York City than at Dartmouth University in quiet Hanover, New Hampshire.
- An underachieving and lazy student at an Ivy League school will likely not go as far as a top student and leader from a non-Ivy school.
- A student will achieve where he can thrive; not every student will do best in any one or every one of the Ivies' cultures and atmospheres. Attending an Ivy is not a guarantee of future success: Academic superstars, political and business leaders, prizewinning scientists and artists have attended—and may be teaching at—a wide range of colleges across the country.

THANK-YOU CARDS REALLY leave a positive impression. After any sort of meeting with a college representative, I made sure to get their contact information. Once at home, I immediately sat down and wrote an eloquent and complimentary thank-you letter while our meeting was still fresh in my mind. College representatives keep all these thank-you notes on file.

—*Brittany Ryan*
Dallas, Texas
University of Oklahoma

• • • • • • • •

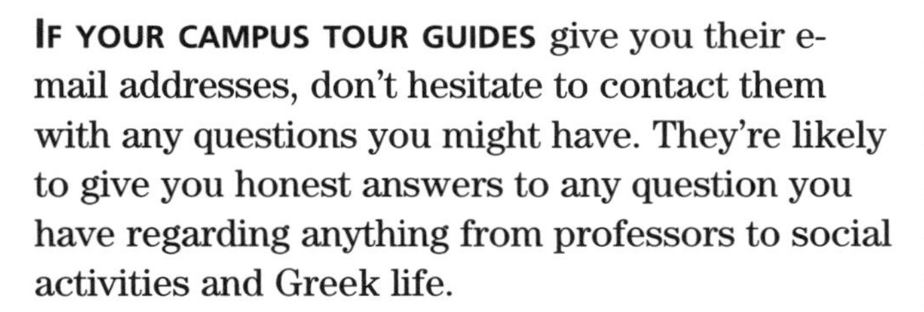

IF YOUR CAMPUS TOUR GUIDES give you their e-mail addresses, don't hesitate to contact them with any questions you might have. They're likely to give you honest answers to any question you have regarding anything from professors to social activities and Greek life.

—*Amanda Nelson-Duac*
St. Augustine, Florida
George Washington University

• • • • • • • •

I WAS REALLY INTERESTED IN MACALESTER, a college in St. Paul, Minnesota. My mom insisted that if she was going to make the visit with me, we had to visit another college on her list. She chose Knox College from the book *Colleges That Change Lives*. We flew to Chicago and then drove to Knox. From the second I stepped on the campus, I knew this was where I wanted to go. I just felt so comfortable there, more comfortable than at any of the colleges I was looking at. We traveled on to Macalester, and I ended up not liking that school at all. I applied to Knox, knowing it was my first choice, and that is where I chose to go. I have not regretted it in the least.

—*Maren Reisch*
Geneva, New York
Knox College

I DIDN'T CHECK OUT THE SCHOOLS as I was applying; I waited to see where I got in and then started the campus visits. Once I got into Cornell, I attended a special day in April to check it out, to see where I'd be living, to see if I could sit in on some classes, and take tours. That was nice. I saw where the engineering quad was and was able to imagine my life there.

—*ADAM KRESSEL*
MIAMI, FLORIDA
CORNELL UNIVERSITY

A Q-TIP

Ask only open-ended questions of the tour guide, the information session leader, and any students you happen to meet. By asking a question that only requires a "yes" or "no" response, you will not really receive the information you are seeking.

BE CAREFUL WHICH STUDENTS you hang out with on your visit. I visited with this kid to see how he lived and what he did. He made the college seem a helluva lot more interesting than it actually was. He wasn't worried about academics. He had a party lined up every Saturday. He was like, "Oh, you'll learn stuff. It's not too hard." I bought the story, and I attended the college. But now I'm transferring because I don't like it. If I had to do it again, I would try to hook up with more mainstream students to get a clearer picture of what campus life is like.

—*WILLIAM ALVAREZ*
LYNDHURST, NEW JERSEY
RUTGERS UNIVERSITY

SPRING BREAK MY JUNIOR YEAR I visited three schools, and I ended up applying to two. And then I visited a few more during senior year, including the school I chose. At each visit, I stayed on campus to see where I felt most at home, which one provided me with the most opportunities, and which one I saw myself at for the next four years.

—*HALLI LEVY*
SOLON, OHIO
UNIVERSITY OF MISSOURI

HEADS UP: ON VISITING SCHOOLS

Nothing will help you find out where you belong like the college visit: You'll get a good sense of the atmosphere, the culture, the academics, and the experience. You should ultimately choose your school based on this "feel." Explore the campus, ask a lot of questions, and follow these four tips.

- Dress to casually impress. You do not need to dress up, but you should be wearing clothing that covers your body appropriately and is presentable. You never know whom you will meet in the admissions office. Yes, they expect you to be comfortable for the tour and information session, but know that your presentation still counts.

- At some schools, it may be important to make personal contact with your admissions officer. However, if you have nothing to ask, it is better not to have the person called down to the lobby to meet you. It usually leaves a bad impression or no impression at all if you make the officer do all the talking. Know that admissions officers are happy to admit students they have never met.

- If you do see an admissions officer, follow up with a thank-you note—an e-mail is fine—thank-you for his or her time. This is a gesture that shows your continued interest—and it is the polite thing to do.

- Pay attention and jot down impressions immediately on the way home. Some schools ask for a "Why are you applying here?" essay, and your visits will give you material for the essay.

OTHER SIDE OF THE DESK: LOOKING AT YOURSELF THE WAY AO'S SEE YOU

We admire and respect you, but be realistic:

- You may be a big fish in your community, but compared to other big fish, you may not be so big.
- It is *very* hard these days to do anything truly unique that an AO has not seen, so don't feel pressure to be unique.

TOUR ANY COLLEGE CAMPUS that you are interested in. You get an entirely different feel for the school when you pull your head out of college books and Web pages and walk around the campus. I knew when I walked on the Wake Forest campus that it was where I wanted to be. Something about being there felt right, a feeling you cannot get looking at any staged picture on a brochure or reading any statistics.

—*Whitney Tritt*
Atlanta, Georgia
Wake Forest University

I WISH I HAD VISITED ONE SCHOOL that was pretty far from home. I limited myself to schools that were within about three hours from home. But I later realized that in many ways they were all very similar. Just for a different perspective, I wish I had taken a trip to a school in Michigan or Missouri just to get a sampling of how things could be different.

—*Burt Emmet*
Newark, Delaware
University of Delaware

I VISITED ALL THE CAMPUSES that I applied to. If possible, you should stay with someone you know at the school, or have the school arrange for you to stay with a student. In my case, I had sent in my deposit to another school that I thought I loved. But when I stayed with a friend of mine, I had the most miserable time and I ended up not going. Then I stayed with a friend at my current school and I had an *amazing* time. It helped me decide on which school I wanted to spend the next four years at.

—*MATT BORTNICK*
EAST BRUNSWICK, NEW JERSEY
INDIANA UNIVERSITY

ONE OF THE MOST IMPORTANT THINGS to look at when visiting a college campus is how people live. What you want is real, candid views from students who attend the school. The day-to-day routine of students will give you an idea of what to expect if you decide to go to the school. It's also an interesting insight into how they've adjusted to the school themselves.

—*MAILE CERIZO*
MAUI, HAWAII
POINT LOMA NAZARENE UNIVERSITY

FOLLOW UP YOUR VISIT TO A COLLEGE with a call to the school at least once a week. With my college, I called at least three times a week until I was admitted. The counselor later told me that as soon as she would hear "hello" on the other line, she knew it was me. I was very proactive. She told me that I showed her that I would not stop until I reached my goal. I was going to do whatever I had to do to get in.

—*DIANE KOTCHEY*
FREDONIA, NEW YORK
STATE UNIVERSITY OF NEW YORK, UNIVERSITY AT BUFFALO

My daughter probably wishes she had visited more schools. As a parent, I think 10 to 12 campus visits are plenty!

—*DEBBIE*
PITTSBURGH, PENNSYLVANIA
P OHIO UNIVERSITY

I DID A UNIVERSITY-SPONSORED VISIT with my parents, and a visit with friends; both are a good idea. If I just relied on my friends, I'd only get a feel for the social scene (which was fun to experience, too!).

—*JESSICA NEWMAN*
WEST BLOOMFIELD, MICHIGAN
MICHIGAN STATE UNIVERSITY

“During the interviews, make sure people are being level with you when they're talking about the school. Keep saying, ‘No, seriously ...’ until you get them to really talk honestly about the ups and the downs.”

—*KATHRYN*
PHILADELPHIA, PENNSYLVANIA
SARAH LAWRENCE COLLEGE

BEING ON THE CAMPUS LETS you see what you're getting into. I went to one college I'd been pretty interested in, but the people I met were unfriendly and the campus was really ugly. I realized I could never be happy there for four years; that's something you're not going to figure out by reading the brochures.

—*EMILY ROSE*
ATLANTA, GEORGIA
AGNES SCOTT COLLEGE

OTHER SIDE OF THE DESK: A JOB FOR HOLMES AND WATSON

AOs are talented detectives—very few students can fool them. Because they read hundreds, or sometimes thousands, of applications each year, they easily spot exaggeration or insincerity in applications.

UNC WAS MY FIRST CHOICE FOR COLLEGE. As the May 1st deadline approached, however, I had a typical panic over making such a huge decision. I made my parents fly with me to Nashville to visit Vanderbilt; I had never seen the campus and wanted to make sure that I was making the right decision. However, I left Nashville more certain than ever that I wanted to go to UNC.

—*Bethany Black*
Chapel Hill, North Carolina
University of North Carolina

• • • • • • • • •

MY HUSBAND AND I ASKED our daughter if she wanted us to visit the campus with her or if she wanted to go on her own. She decided she wanted to be left there, so I drove her to the admissions office and we made a plan to meet later. My advice to other parents: You're there to help your child debrief during the college admissions process. You don't have to go with them to see everything. You'll be in the way if you're physically with them as they're figuring it out.

—*Nancy Feresten*
Washington, D.C.
P

THE BEST QUESTION I ASKED WAS, "How much reading and writing is assigned in the first year?" I wanted to know this because it would allow me to figure out how many credits I thought I could realistically carry the first year. Don't sign up for 18 credits and then find out that the school is big on tons of reading and writing in the first year.

—SHAUNA VANARDEN
WINCHESTER, VIRGINIA
UNIVERSITY OF VIRGINIA

I looked for an institution in which I could grow academically as well as socially. It is important to keep both factors in mind.

—SCOTT G.
CHESTERFIELD, MISSOURI
UNIVERSITY OF ILLINOIS

SPEND A FEW DAYS IN THE city or town nearest the university. Often campus life is affected by the city or town it's located in or near; if you don't like the city, there's a possibility you won't like the campus.

—AMANDA NELSON-DUAC
ST. AUGUSTINE, FLORIDA
GEORGE WASHINGTON UNIVERSITY

ASK ABOUT THE SOCIAL LIFE when talking to students. What do they do on the weekends? How much do people drink? Is it a big deal if you don't drink? If you're not comfortable with that kind of social life, you might not fit in.

—EMMA
HARRINGTON PARK, NEW JERSEY
BROWN UNIVERSITY

PARENTS, THE STUDENT NEEDS TO VISIT small campuses and large campuses, inner-city and college-town environments. Ask yourself, "Can this child succeed far from home?" Some kids at this age think they want to get as far away from home as possible, but once there, they feel unsure and start questioning their choice.

—SUSAN
YARDLEY, PENNSYLVANIA
P UNIVERSITY OF OKLAHOMA

A FEW WORDS ABOUT VISITS

- **Visiting makes all the difference, one way or the other. If you can't go to the school for economic reasons, do lots of research.**
- **Be aware: A tour guide can make or break a visit and strongly influence your decision.**
- **Statistics indicate that if the weather is bad during a first campus visit, the student probably won't end up choosing that school.**
- **If visiting is not an option, evaluate schools on some basis other than name recognition (which you should be doing anyway).**

—Kerry Keegan, College Admissions Counselor
Academy of the Holy Names, Tampa, Florida

Our son seemed to know by driving through a school whether he wanted to go back for a tour. We drove through at least three schools where he knew right away they weren't for him. At one, he decided instantly because its football stadium "looked like crap."

—K. F.
Basking Ridge, New Jersey
P Lafayette College

The main question I had was, "Can I see myself walking across this quad and talking to these people for the next four years?" When I visited Harvard, it took me about three minutes on the campus before I looked at my father and pleaded with him to get me out of there. Listen to those instincts.

—Catherine Howard
New Orleans, Louisiana
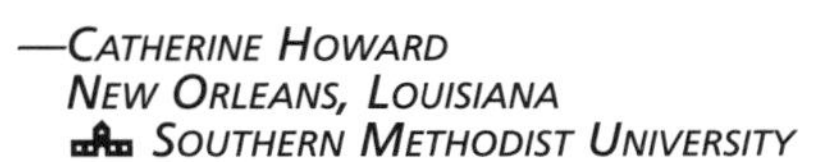
Southern Methodist University

THE SUMMER BEFORE MY SENIOR YEAR, I went on a road trip with my mom to see different campuses. A school may be totally different than you think. St. Mary's College of Maryland was really nice, but when I got there, I realized that it's in the middle of nowhere. I had been thinking about going to American University and planned to visit it. But when I got there, it was too crowded. The visits showed me what the campuses and dorms were like, and what the kids were like.

—*MAREK DUDZIAK*
BAYONNE, NEW JERSEY
LOYOLA COLLEGE

THE REAL STRESSFUL PART was taking trips to the colleges with my parents. Road trips with only your parents aren't fun!

—*ADRIENNE LANG*
OLATHE, KANSAS
TEXAS CHRISTIAN UNIVERSITY

VISIT THE COLLEGE WHEN SCHOOL is in session before making any final decisions; you're going to spend the next four years of your life there! Prospective students should not only look at the buildings when visiting the schools; they should take a look at the students walking around the campus. Do they look happy to be there?

—*ERICA GOLDENBERG*
BLOOMINGTON, INDIANA
INDIANA UNIVERSITY

Bank on It: Scholarships, Financial Aid & Loans

All this talk about getting into the college of your choice, but how are you going to pay for it? The cost of college has risen far faster than inflation in recent years; even in-state tuition can cost more than $10,000 a year. A part-time job delivering pizza just won't cover that. From need-based to merit or athletic scholarships, as well as federal grants and private donations to college education, plenty of options are available. We asked college students to show us the money. Read on for valuable advice.

GET FINANCIAL AID DONE EARLY. As soon as you apply, start the process. There are always forms that are missing or ones that you filled out wrong. If you wait too long to do this, you won't get financial aid.

—*JENNIFER DRAGOVICH*
SEMINOLE, FLORIDA
FLORIDA STATE UNIVERSITY

THE FINANCIAL AID FORMS ARE NOT DIFFICULT. JUST JUMP IN THERE AND DO IT!

—*BETH REINGOLD GLUCK*
ATLANTA, GEORGIA
P UNIVERSITY OF SOUTHERN CALIFORNIA

- Be prepared to be patient; it's just not a quick and easy process.
- Be a good detective: there are scholarships out there, even in your local community.
- The cost adds up, in application fees, but in odd expenses, too—save where you can.
- Work out a budget for school; it's easy to live beyond your means.
- Negotiate: Schools can be more flexible than you think.

BE WILLING TO REALLY WORK on financial aid if you need to. A kid from my hometown got about $100,000 in aid by winning a ton of smaller scholarships that he found on *Fastweb.com.*

—*KAYLEIGH SHEBS*
AMBRIDGE, PENNSYLVANIA
AGNES SCOTT COLLEGE

PARENTS, YOU HAVE TO GET your tax information together much sooner than you're used to. Every school has a different date for financial aid forms, and if you miss it, tough. We had to have our taxes done at the beginning of February, which was a really big change for us.

—*M.B.*
MINNEAPOLIS, MINNESOTA
P UNIVERSITY OF MICHIGAN

TALK TO THE FINANCIAL AID COUNSELORS as soon as you arrive at your college. Try to build a relationship with one of them. This will be important, especially when you start applying for new or renewed scholarships or grants. I regularly discuss deadlines and payment plans with my counselor. The last thing you want to worry about as a college student is payment deadlines.

—*MAILE CERIZO*
MAUI, HAWAII
POINT LOMA NAZARENE UNIVERSITY

THERE ARE ENDOWMENTS that fund literally millions of scholarships. Don't just browse the Internet for full rides. Take the time to write essays for the smaller $500 and $1,000 scholarships. First, they add up quickly. Second, once you write a couple of essays, you'll find there is a pretty straightforward model to most application processes. Once you write four or five letters, you can make little changes and send them to other groups. This expedites the process and gives you a much better chance of getting the scholarships.

—*DOMINIC BERARDI*
CINCINNATI, OHIO
UNIVERSITY OF CINCINNATI

Application fees suck! An extra $50 adds up so fast.

—*ANONYMOUS*
DECATUR, GEORGIA
AGNES SCOTT COLLEGE

TOP FIVE COLLEGE FINANCIAL BLUNDERS

1. Not applying for aid
2. Saving in a child's name
3. Missing scholarships
4. Sending in forms too late
5. Paying financial planners to do it

APPLY FOR EVERY SCHOLARSHIP POSSIBLE. Need-based money is great because you don't have to pay it back and there are usually low GPA requirements. Watch out for merit-based scholarships that require 3.5 or 3.3 GPAs. College GPAs are not like high school: they're much harder to maintain or raise.

—*SARAH BORMEL*
BALTIMORE, MARYLAND
BOSTON UNIVERSITY

> "Saving up before going to a college was a really good idea. Even if you just take less than half out of what you earn from baby-sitting or doing the odd job, it really adds up and comes in handy in the long run."

—*ELANA SYRTASH*
TORONTO, ONTARIO
STERN COLLEGE

APPLY FOR WORK-STUDY OR ASSISTANTSHIPS right after you are accepted to have a better chance at getting the most sought-after jobs. These positions often pay a portion or all of your tuition, and include a stipend for spending money.

—*CASEY BOND*
GRAND RAPIDS, MICHIGAN
GRAND VALLEY STATE UNIVERSITY

ROOM TO NEGOTIATE?

BE PERSISTENT. I was accepted to Agnes Scott but needed more money, so my dad kept calling the swim coach and saying, “You know, my daughter would really like to swim for your team, but we need help.” That worked; they increased my scholarship.

—DANA NOTESTINE
EAST POINT, GEORGIA
AGNES SCOTT COLLEGE

• • • • • • • •

DON’T LET THE MONEY STAND IN THE WAY. You don’t have to accept the first package a college gives you; keep reapplying. Schools that supposedly won’t give you anything usually try to find a way to get you in if you’ve been accepted.

—HANNAH ASSADI
SCOTTSDALE, ARIZONA
COLUMBIA COLLEGE

• • • • • • • •

THEY TELL YOU THAT YOU CAN NEGOTIATE YOUR FINANCIAL AID. My experience is that it’s not the case. I tried to negotiate with MIT and they weren’t having it. The good schools are less willing to negotiate because they have so many applicants. I ended up going to Villanova, but even the little bit I tried to push them, they really wouldn’t budge. My general feeling is that the negotiating process is overrated.

—DAVID
NEWARK, DELAWARE
VILLANOVA UNIVERSITY

OTHER SIDE OF THE DESK: IMPROVING YIELD WITH SCHOLARSHIPS AND LOANS

Schools that offer merit aid or merit scholarships do so to try to yield the students they most want and love. Some scholarships are awarded for measurable GPA or SAT criteria, and some are awarded for more intangible reasons, such as "leadership" or "talent." Recipients are often selected by committees and AO recommendations, so there is some element of randomness in this process, too; many deserving candidates will not receive this aid.

FASTWEB.COM IS BY FAR the best resource available to young students looking for free money. I applied for more than 10 different independent grants and scholarships through this site. There is literally a scholarship for everyone if you look hard enough. I was very active in community service, for instance, and received $10,000 from the Toyota Motor Company. Many companies offer grants such as this, so take advantage of them. The biggest mistake of the admissions process often comes through overlooking the immense financial opportunities available to incoming students. Also, fafsa.ed.gov is the site for federal financial aid. Always fill out a FAFSA. It's an important element of your application, regardless of your current financial standing. You may get more grant money than you anticipate.

—*Lauren Elizabeth Leahy*
Dallas, Texas
Southern Methodist University

MY FAMILY WASN'T REALLY there for me financially, so I didn't have anyone when I was applying telling me, "Go into debt if you need to; it'll pay off in the long run." If I had it all to do over again, I would have focused more on where an education could get me, not how much it would cost.

—MARY PERALTA
BATON ROUGE, LOUISIANA
LOUISIANA STATE UNIVERSITY

IF I COULD DO ANYTHING DIFFERENT, I would have demanded more help and guidance with financial aid. Although my memories of Seton Hill are very fond, it was not the school I should have chosen, financially speaking. I am in severe debt due to my education. At the time, I didn't care how much school would cost; I just wanted to make sure I could get in. Figure out ahead of time how you're going to pay for your education later on!

—JODI
PITTSBURGH, PENNSYLVANIA
SETON HILL UNIVERSITY

I got a scholarship to York University, so I accepted because it was better than the others!

—MICHAEL NOBLE
TORONTO, ONTARIO
YORK UNIVERSITY

UNUSUAL SCHOLARSHIPS

- The United Daughters of the Confederacy offers $400–$1,500 in scholarships to lineal descendants of Confederate soldiers.
- Harness Tracks of America offers $2,500–$3,000 in scholarships to students who are actively involved in harness racing.
- Two/Ten International Footwear Foundation offers up to $2,000 in scholarships to children of workers in the footwear industry.

I BECAME BORDERLINE OBSESSED with applying for scholarships. Fastweb.com is a great Web site that provides much information on many scholarships. I can't even remember how many scholarships I applied for. At the end of it all, I was a finalist for some scholarships and even managed to schedule interviews for some. Though I did not make the final cut on many of them, the entire process was a good learning experience that taught me excellent essay-writing and interviewing skills. Also realize that colleges have many scholarships out there just waiting to be seized by willing students. I ended up with three different, significant scholarships from OU alone. Not only did they provide me with considerable scholarship money, but they also gave me some sort of prestigious title that will be regarded highly on campus.

—*Brittany Ryan*
Dallas, Texas
University of Oklahoma

UNLESS YOU ARE FINANCIALLY SECURE or want to get into a school that is way out of reach, I would not recommend early decision.

—*Sarah Bormel*
Baltimore, Maryland
Boston University

CALLING IN THE FEDS

The Free Application for Federal Student Aid (FAFSA) is mandatory if you'll be applying for any federal financial aid. The FAFSA Web site is www.ed.gov/offices/OPE/express.htm.

FAME: THE AUDITION

I had to compete for my dance scholarship. The audition was the most stressful part of the process. Coming face-to-face with your competition is something every dancer must deal with. I had to learn to stay focused in those tense situations, remain calm, and have confidence in my own talent. Staying true to your passion is the most crucial part of the whole process. Rejections will come and they certainly did for me, but this did not stop me from believing that dance was something I needed to pursue.

—*Jennifer Keys*
Baltimore, Maryland
New York University

School list servers can be a valuable source of financial aid information. Check out your school's listserv for scholarship and leadership opportunities. For some reason, students aren't interested in them; they just delete them, and don't bother to read them. That's a mistake if you are looking for money.

—*Josh Gellers*
New York, New York
University of Florida

My guidance counselor directed me to some scholarships, but I found a lot more online. It's just a matter of finding them and applying. From my experience, the more you get involved in while in high school and the more varied the activities you are involved in, the more you'll have opportunities to find scholarships that you are eligible for.

—*Julie Collins*
Des Moines, Iowa
Drake University

ATHLETIC SCHOLARSHIPS

IF YOU'RE AN ATHLETE AND WANT TO PLAY ON A COLLEGE TEAM, arrange a meeting with the coach. Bring your scrapbook, statistics, or other information that will help give a clear picture of your talents. Consider asking your high school coach to send a letter to the college on your behalf. As soon as I met with the baseball coach, I knew we were going to be able to work well together. I don't think you can be sure of something like that until you meet face-to-face. He put my mind at ease about some concerns I had.

—Brian Snider
Youngstown, Ohio
Youngstown State University

WHEN YOU'RE AN ATHLETE LOOKING FOR A SCHOOL, you have to market yourself. I was in the newspaper; I was first team all-state and played on select teams. I sent profiles to universities to tell them what I had accomplished; I was recruited by several colleges. I went to the school that offered me the most money, a full scholarship. It was all about the money: who was going to give me the most.

—Andrew
Dearborn, Michigan
Wayne State University

I HAD A COACH IN BASKETBALL WHO HAD BEEN AN ALL-AMERICAN, so he had been through the recruiting thing. I had many questions, and it was nice to be able to turn to him. Even if your coach wasn't recruited, chances are that you are not the first athlete he or she had who was recruited. So ask the coach for help.

—Linda Roadarmel
Parkersburg, West Virginia

SOME WEB SITES, such as msn.com, have really helpful tuition calculators that give you a very realistic and personal idea of what college will cost. It allows you to enter your state, and in some cases even your school as well as other personal information, so that you really know what to expect. After I did the calculations there, I found that it was going to cost me about $1,500 more per year than I was figuring. And that amount is nothing to sneeze at for a student.

—TABITHA HAGAR
WILMINGTON, DELAWARE
UNIVERSITY OF DELAWARE

FINANCIALLY, IT HELPS THAT OUR DAUGHTER is working. It's just in a coffee shop, but in addition to making some money, it really motivates her and helps her organize her time. And since the coffee house has wireless technology, she can do all her homework there and hang out with her friends. It's been a big benefit all around.

—M.B.
MINNEAPOLIS, MINNESOTA
P UNIVERSITY OF MICHIGAN

DON'T FORGET, as I did, that work-study wages are subject to state and federal withholding taxes and Medicare. Once you deduct those amounts, work-study may not seem like such a good idea. I had pretty much my whole first check spent already in my mind before I got it. Then I was pretty disappointed to find out that taxes were going to come out of it. Keep that in mind when trying to figure out if work-study is worth it to you.

—KEN KEEL
WINCHESTER, VIRGINIA
UNIVERSITY OF VIRGINIA

FINANCIAL FACTOID

Student loans surpassed grants as the primary form of financial aid for undergrads. Federal loans come in three types: Perkins, Stafford, and PLUS (Parent Loan for Undergraduate Students).

WHEN IT COMES TO SCHOLARSHIPS, always go for it. My college gave me a full ride in theater. I was quite lucky to get it. I had applied for it two months after they had already done the auditions for it. I begged the professor to give me a shot. He let me audition, and as it turned out, they liked me and they gave me the full ride. I really needed it.

—*HEIDI*
YERINGTON, MAINE
TEXAS SOUTHERN UNIVERSITY

• • • • • • • •

"My dad offered to give me the difference in tuition if I chose a less expensive school. I was expected to go to Washington University, but UC Berkeley is much less expensive."

—*DANIEL J. SEIGLE*
WEST DUNDEE, ILLINOIS
UNIVERSITY OF CALIFORNIA, BERKELEY

• • • • • • • •

APPLYING FOR FEDERAL STUDENT loans is a very confusing and painful process. The forms are impossible, and if I didn't have my dad helping me, I would never have figured them out. One thing I learned, though, is that the phone number on the FAFSA application is very useful. The customer service people there are very helpful, even when you call them 100 times.

—*ANONYMOUS*
LOS ANGELES, CALIFORNIA
UNIVERSITY OF CALIFORNIA, LOS ANGELES

WHEN COLLEGE ADMISSION GOES SWIMMINGLY

In many ways, being recruited for my swimming helped me bypass a lot of the trouble my friends went through: applying to 12 different schools, getting turned down by their top choices, or having to wait until the spring to decide which school to go to. I had to base my decision not only on factors such as academics, location, and social scene, but also on the strength of the athletic department, the coaches, and the swim team. This helped me whittle down my list. My top two priorities were academics and athletic reputation, so when college coaches started calling me before my senior year, I had about eight schools I was still interested in.

While some may think that getting calls from coaches and getting flown out to schools around the country is glamorous, it's also pretty stressful. First, I had no idea if my top-choice schools would call me. No call means no recruiting trip. On the other hand, turning down coaches who called from schools I had no interest in was also nerve-racking. I ended up taking four recruiting trips in the fall of my senior year: Harvard, Yale, Princeton, and Stanford. That fall, I felt as if I was always traveling. I would fly out Thursday night and fly home early Sunday morning.

I had sent in my Stanford application and been accepted by mid-October. After taking my trip, I knew it was the school for me. Everything from the academics to the swim team to the amazing weather made the choice clear to me. I signed a letter of intent in November, which was nice because I got to wear my college sweatshirt while all my friends were sweating getting their letters.

—*Katherine Bell*
Stanford, California
Stanford University

HEADS UP: FINANCIAL AID

Your financial situation will dictate how much colleges can help you. If you and your family have little money, schools can be very generous with financial aid and scholarship money, and private schools can be just as affordable as public schools. There are two financial aid processes you need to complete—one for the national aid, filling out a CSS-PROFILE form, which is obtainable in your high school; and one for the school-specific aid, obtainable from the schools themselves with the admissions applications.

TIP: Some private schools will not tie admission to financial aid requirements, but some will. You will find *need-blind schools*, in which the admissions committees make decisions without seeing financial aid forms and without considering financial situation, and *need-aware* or *need-sensitive schools*, in which a portion of their admissions hinges on ability to pay. This usually occurs with the last candidates in the pool and will vary by school. Ask your prospective schools if they are need-blind or need-sensitive.

TIP: Apply for aid even if you suspect you may not qualify for it. Colleges take into account many factors you may not realize, such as the number of your siblings in college, as well as assets and income tax forms. Families making $100,000 or more can still qualify for aid. If you do not apply for aid at the outset, you are usually unable to apply for aid at a later date.

MERIT AID: To boost enrollment of the top portion of their applicant pool, some schools will offer merit scholarships on top of need-based aid. Merit scholarships are monies granted—no payback required—as a reward for a strong and interesting academic or extracurricular profile.

GET HELP FROM YOUR HIGH SCHOOL. Perhaps because my husband passed away in my daughter's sophomore year, her school's administration and faculty were exceptionally caring. They knew her strengths and weaknesses and clearly knew our financial limitations. Therefore, I was surprised when many of her advisers strongly urged her to apply to Sarah Lawrence College. It seemed odd to try for such a high-end school, since we couldn't afford for her to "accept an acceptance" if she succeeded. When we asked about our economic concerns, all her advisers had the same response: First, show them you belong there; then ask them how to make that happen! I guess they got the big picture we were missing. They pushed hard for her.

—*MICKIE MANDEL*
RIVERDALE, NEW YORK
P SARAH LAWRENCE COLLEGE

• • • • • • • •

A MAIN REASON I stayed in my home state of Michigan was financial. I didn't want to put my parents through more expenses, and there are good schools here. I'm getting financial aid and I got student loans, and that's how we're paying for college now.

—*JESSICA NEWMAN*
WEST BLOOMFIELD, MICHIGAN
MICHIGAN STATE UNIVERSITY

• • • • • • • •

GO FOR IT, WHETHER YOU THINK you'll get it or not. Apply for those $1,000 and $2,000 scholarships for writing a paper. I know people who have gotten a few of those, which added up to $5,000. That's a good amount of money to help pay for college.

—*TRENT*
GRAPEVINE, TEXAS
UNIVERSITY OF COLORADO

Get your parents' help when applying for financial aid. It's really confusing. I did part of it, but it wasn't something I could do on my own.

—*WILLIAM ALVAREZ*
LYNDHURST, NEW JERSEY
RUTGERS UNIVERSITY

A FEW WORDS OF ADVICE

College debt is real debt. Six to nine months after graduation, you'd better be prepared for a chunk of your income to go toward paying it off. Before taking an admissions offer to an expensive school, think long and hard about whether student loans are worth it for you.

Work out a budget for yourself. It's way too easy to live beyond your means in college.

—*Daniel*
Wheeling, West Virginia
Columbia University

All you hear when you're applying is, "Don't worry about the money," but that's not always the best advice. I didn't realize how much that debt would affect my life. Now I'm about to graduate, and I'm facing all these loans. You have to wonder, was it worth it?

—*Anonymous*
Decatur, Georgia
Agnes Scott College

Get on Fastweb! The site is able to find lots of scholarships. Apply for as many things as you can, even the little scholarships. Get online and search for scholarships. If you are Native American, African American or any kind of minority, there are all kinds of organizations and businesses that offer scholarships for you; you have to make the effort to find them.

—*Josiah White*
Carrollton, Texas
Oklahoma Baptist University

THE SQUEAKY WHEEL GETS THE GREASE: Call, complain, do what you need to do to get scholarship money and financial aid. I originally received no scholarship money from USC, but my father made a couple of phone calls (having no connections to anyone important at the university), and I received in the mail a $4,000 annual scholarship, which was pretty neat!

—*DAVID LICHTENSTEIN*
SAN DIEGO, CALIFORNIA
UNIVERSITY OF SOUTHERN CALIFORNIA

THE FAFSA APPLICATION can be found on the Web site www.fafsa.ed.gov. But be careful, there are many Web sites out there designed to look like the FAFSA site, but which require a money deposit. I was very close to falling for one of these scams, initially believing that a down payment was required. Any scholarship or financial aid scholarship that asks for money is illegitimate.

—*BRITTANY RYAN*
DALLAS, TEXAS
UNIVERSITY OF OKLAHOMA

I have a friend who got a disability scholarship because of being color-blind!

—*RACHANN N. MCKNIGHT*
HOUSTON, TEXAS
INDIANA UNIVERSITY

FOR AID, LOOK WITHIN

Director David (*Blue Velvet*) Lynch has formed the Foundation for Consciousness-Based Education and World Peace to encourage students to deal with stress through meditation. He awarded $2,500 in vouchers for TM classes, and those who did not receive an award can apply for a loan through Citibank arranged by Maharishi University, at 7 percent interest!

APPLY FOR EVERY SCHOLARSHIP; it helps. Also, don't stop once you're in college. I've received a second scholarship from TCU the past few semesters because of my work in my department.

—*Adrienne Lang*
Olathe, Kansas
Texas Christian University

"Jump on every cent they will give you. I had too much pride to take advantage of the fact that I am from an underrepresented minority. I'm over that now."

—*Seth*
Sunnyvale, California
University of California, Berkeley

AS AN ATHLETE, the most important thing to do in the beginning is to put yourself out there, sell yourself. I sent out e-mails and my personal player profile (stats and measurements) to a list of maybe 50 schools I was potentially interested in. I felt this type of sharing my abilities would contradict my modesty, but in the end I learned it is all part of the game. Put yourself out there and make sure the coaches or schools in general know how serious you are about attending the school. If there are opportunities for a meeting or interviews at any point, by all means take them!

—*Jackie Adlam*
Mill Valley, California
Colgate University

I KNOW THAT I'M NOT GETTING a lot of financial aid from the state, because my parents can afford college. I'm doing my best to find outside scholarships. I'll soon know my high school class ranking, which determines what financial aid the college will give me. Being at the top of the class, or being valedictorian or salutatorian, has an impact as well. I applied for several different scholarships: Comcast is giving me one, as is the high school (for community service), and I've applied for theater scholarships. There's a lot you can apply for.

—*Jessie Schoren*
Lindenwold, New Jersey
Rowan University

DOUBLE THE FUN

A number of colleges offer scholarships or discounts for twins and triplets:

- **Carl Albert State College in Oklahoma (Paula Nieto Twin Scholarship)**
- **George Washington University in Washington, D.C. (50 percent discount for second sibling)**
- **Lake Erie College in Painesville, Ohio (each twin gets the scholarship in alternate years)**
- **Morris Brown College, Atlanta, Georgia**
- **Northeastern Oklahoma A&M College**
- **Randolph-Macon Women's College, Lynchburg, Virginia (15 percent discount)**
- **Sterling College in Kansas (50 percent discount for each twin)**
- **West Chester University of Pennsylvania (Bonnie Evans Feinberg Scholarship)**

DON'T WASTE YOUR MONEY by allowing your child to apply to schools that you know you cannot afford or will not allow your child to attend. This will only set them up for disappointment. Set your child up for success.

—*Meryl Sher*
Weston, Florida
P University of Florida

"Every college has a financial aid office. They offer all kinds of weird aid. Apply to all that you can. The Hastings Milledge Grant for Left-Handed Republican Narcoleptics has your name all over it."

—*Adam Dreyfus*
San Francisco, California
University of Connecticut

I HAVE TWO JOBS TO HELP PAY for my education. I pay for 75 percent of my schooling, and my dad pays the rest, so I feel a big difference from high school. If I screw up, it's my problem. I'm jealous of people who have their parents pay for school, sometimes they take advantage: they drink, they skip classes. I take it seriously.

—*Michael Abramovitz*
Tucson, Arizona
University of Arizona

I CHOSE CALIFORNIA STATE UNIVERSITY, Fresno because I earned the Smittcamp Family Honors College full-ride scholarship. Out of 575 seniors in the Central Valley, only 50 to 75 are chosen for this prestigious academic scholarship. My parents could not afford to send me to college; an English teacher told me about this program, and said it was for any senior who wants to go straight into college at Fresno State. It was an academic scholarship, meaning you usually have to get pretty good grades. But it is also based on merit, need, and community involvement. The program paid for my tuition, campus room, parking, an iBook laptop and printer, a book stipend, and other perks. Best of all, I could live "away from home" and still be near my family and friends in Fresno.

—*EMILY TUCK*
FRESNO, CALIFORNIA
CALIFORNIA STATE UNIVERSITY

GET YOUR TAXES DONE EARLY so you can complete the financial aid papers by the deadline. Always follow up to make sure they were processed.

—*KIM MOORE*
OCEANSIDE, CALIFORNIA
P INDIANA UNIVERSITY

I HAVE A COUPLE OF RANDOM scholarships from outside organizations; they mostly cover costs of books. There's probably a scholarship out there for everyone. When I was searching, I think I found one that applied to left-handed California female students of eastern European descent with a GPA of 3.0 or above in a public school. Or something like that. Not even kidding.

—*JESSICA*
SARATOGA, CALIFORNIA
UNIVERSITY OF SOUTHERN CALIFORNIA

Look for additional scholarships online. Even those $500 or $1,000 scholarships, if you get three or more of them, add up.

—*DANE SKILBRED*
SAINT PAUL, MINNESOTA
SANTA CLARA UNIVERSITY

National scholarships are fine and dandy, but you're competing against a nation of kids. There are many businesses in your community that give out scholarships to local kids. Those are to your advantage, because not only do you have a better chance of getting them, but you can actually get more of them. I had a friend who got more than $24,000 in local scholarships because she applied for every single one.

—Mar-y-Sol
Martindale, Texas
Texas State University

• • • • • • • •

When I received my acceptance letter from Ithaca College, I celebrated by running around and screaming. I celebrated until I got to the second page, detailing the financial aid I was to be given, and then my heart sank. Although I had a 97 average in high school and strong extracurricular activities, I wasn't being offered much financial aid, and that meant I had to choose another college.

—Jason Torreano
Lockport, New York
State University of New York, Brockport

• • • • • • • •

The financial aid process is brutal but well worth it. Be prepared to fill out more forms than you'll believe. I honestly think they try to break your will by asking for the same information over and over. Just know going in that it's not an easy or a quick process. But if you get aid, it is a big help. My freshman year I got about $3,000 in free money, so I thought all the paperwork was well worth the effort.

—C.L.
New Middletown, Ohio
Youngstown State University

Help! Getting Support From Counselors & Parents

Few things can cause family arguments like the college admissions process. Even so, it is possible for parents and their almost-adult children to work together to ensure the process has a successful outcome. We asked students and parents for advice on this topic. We also asked them about the importance of guidance counselors and private admissions counselors. We realize you're probably receiving advice from most or all of the above. But please read on: We really want what's best for you.

MY PARENTS, SPECIFICALLY MY MOTHER, felt it necessary to repeatedly remind me how many days I had left until the applications were due! Her pressure helped me realize that I really needed to get started on the process (although I believe that I would have completed them anyway).

—*Nathaniel Cohen*
West Hartford, Connecticut
New York University

LET YOUR PARENTS HELP. TWO OR THREE MINDS ARE BETTER THAN ONE!

—*Lauren Sher*
Gainesville, Florida
University of Florida

- Give teachers and counselors a "brag sheet" to help them make you look good.
- It's your job to make sure people send letters and transcripts; make sure it gets done.
- Be clear with your parents; let them know when you need more help, or less.
- Remember, two (or three, or four) heads are better than one.
- Politeness counts: thank those who helped you with a card or gift.

USE YOUR TEACHERS AND COUNSELORS to help you. Our dean helped us out with college admissions. He gave us books to read and talked to us about schools we were interested in. He helped me write my essay. And he also helped me get recommendations from my teachers.

—*Adam Johnson*
Libertyville, Illinois
Western Illinois University

ASK FOR HELP AND IF YOU DON'T GET IT, take initiative. Call your school and be a pain in the ass, because you will definitely benefit from it. Ask questions even if they are the most ridiculous questions you have ever thought of.

—*Tillie*
Houston, Texas
Chatham College

AT THE BEGINNING OF YOUR SENIOR YEAR, it is your responsibility to meet with each teacher you will ask for a recommendation. You should give them an addressed and stamped envelope and all the required forms. It is also helpful to provide a "brag sheet" so they have a complete view of your achievements and activities outside their classroom. One of my teachers told me that she had no idea how involved I was in my church and wouldn't have known to include that information in her letter if it wasn't on the brag sheet.

—EILEEN DAILY
FREDERICK, MARYLAND
EAST CHRISTIAN COLLEGE

THE WORST PART WAS that I felt as if I was by myself in the search process. At my high school, if you weren't interested in the stereotypical big state school, you were pretty much on your own. Our guidance counselors tried to be helpful, but they were pretty clueless. I had to figure out a lot by word of mouth and the Internet.

—A.M.
DECATUR, GEORGIA
AGNES SCOTT COLLEGE

DON'T BE AFRAID TO LOOK STUPID. Ask questions of your teachers and especially of your guidance counselors. I'd ask them, "What would you do if you were me? Where would you go to school if you were me? What did you do wrong during the process that you wish you could do over?" Most kids are afraid of looking dumb by asking a lot of questions. But everyone working at your high school already has a college degree, which means that at one time they were standing exactly where you are now.

—PAMALA BURNSWORTH
MORGANTOWN, WEST VIRGINIA
WEST VIRGINIA UNIVERSITY

Hire an outside expert to help with the application. It was the single smartest thing we did.

—LINDA SALAZAR
PALOS VERDES, CALIFORNIA
P BROOKS INSTITUTE OF PHOTOGRAPHY

SUCH A GOOD BOY

The most important person to rely on when you're going through the college application process and the transition is Mom. This is how I relied on her:

- To teach me how to cook mac and cheese.
- To teach me how to dress, as she did for years.
- To teach me about dating and how to kiss girls (very important in college).
- To teach me how to take notes in class (she's a great notetaker).

Finally, I wish I could've taken my mom with me to school so she could be my wingwoman. My mom's great at picking up gals. I know she would brag to college girls about how great I am. Don't underestimate your parents: They're older and wiser.

—*Daniel*
Toronto, Ontario
York University

The stress is in applying to all the schools. But after a while, you'll start to realize that you'll be able to use the answers to the essay questions over and over again. Just start early, well before the deadline!

—*Lauren Marciniak*
Burr Ridge, Illinois
Bradley University

Every time you're tempted to give a piece of advice to your kid on applying to school, bite your tongue. Let your child think about what he or she wants. I don't listen to that advice, but it *should* open up more conversation!

—*Wendy Lukehart*
Takoma Park, Maryland
P

AT OUR SCHOOL, YOU TOLD THE COUNSELOR who you wanted to be your recommenders, and the counselor approached them and they agreed or disagreed. The counselor's office would send out the applications, and they would add the recommendations as they got them. In this way, we didn't have to bother the teachers, and the applications always got out on time.

—*David*
Newark, Delaware
Villanova University

"Parents, soften 'advice' with a short IM or e-mail. It takes the 'in your face' aspect away from the communication."

—*Beth Reingold Gluck*
Atlanta, Georgia
P University of Southern California

WE WENT TO AN OUTSIDE, private-school adviser who was very helpful and offered a lot of information that we were unaware of until our meeting. He was organized and clearly had years of concrete experience to draw from. The adviser from our school was overburdened, impatient, and gave deadlines that kept changing. I never felt she had an overview of the schools—or perhaps more important, strong connections that could be helpful. I think outside help in our case was useful. Get referrals for advisers from other parents.

—*Anonymous*
Brooklyn, New York
P Purchase College,
State University of New York

PARENT TO PARENT

BE DILIGENT. STAY ON TOP OF THE SITUATION. Work with your children, not against them. Guide them but don't force them. This is one of those situations where parents have to earn their keep. This is a real test of parenthood. Don't screw it up.

—COLLEEN BAKEY
FREDERICK, MARYLAND
P GEORGETOWN UNIVERSITY

• • • • • • • •

MY CHILD'S SCHOOL EMPHASIZED THAT THERE IS A SCHOOL for every kid out there, and that is absolutely true! Parents, don't get caught up with other parents who panic and stress out. Find parents who have been through the process with their older kids, because they tend to be more relaxed about the whole experience. And the more that parents can stay away from the "keeping up with so-and-so" game, the more they can support their child in making a choice that suits his personality and academic level, and help their child feel good about his decisions.

—LINDA SALAZAR
PALOS VERDES, CALIFORNIA
P BROOKS INSTITUTE OF PHOTOGRAPHY

• • • • • • • •

I WASN'T ALWAYS SUCCESSFUL IN STEPPING BACK, but my daughter was not shy about letting me know that I had already given her my opinion and she didn't need to hear it again. My daughter had gone to her grandparents' home in Florida for a week prior to the start of her senior year. She did not complete her applications before going, which she had promised to do. When I called her about it, she got so mad she said she was not coming back home, was going to stay in Florida, and wasn't going to college. Obviously, things calmed down, but that let me know I needed to back off.

—R.F.
ATLANTA, GEORGIA
P UNIVERSITY OF PENNSYLVANIA

HERE'S THE IRONY: After the offers, the accepted-student days, the commitments—in other words, by June of my daughter's senior year—my entire point of view had changed. I could now clearly see that her results were in order with her grades and scores, gender, academic interest, geographic location—and effort. When my friend Jeanne's son began the process, I applied what I knew to his case and told her to relax, he'd do fine. And, in fact, I called eight out of nine of his applications correctly: He was wait-listed at one school I thought he'd get into. But if there'd been a pool, I would've won.

—ANONYMOUS
NEW YORK, NEW YORK
P CARLETON COLLEGE

I STAYED TOTALLY OUT OF MY DAUGHTER'S DECISION about where to go. I didn't even give an opinion, especially since she was considering the college that I attended. Since that college was close to our town, I felt that any enthusiasm that I showed for University of Oklahoma would appear to be self-serving. Actually, keeping my mouth shut was easy because she never considered any other school; in fact, she never even applied to any other school. I do feel good, though, knowing that the decision was hers and that I didn't try to influence her.

—JAYNE ROBERTS
EDMOND, OKLAHOMA
P UNIVERSITY OF OKLAHOMA

MY PARENTS TOOK ME to college campuses to visit, motivated me to sit through yet another admission presentation and campus tour, helped correct my essays, and provided me with constructive criticism. They provided me with SAT classes and a private counselor for one session. They gave me the tools, and I used them; this is how I believe all parents should interact with their children during the admissions process.

—*David Lichtenstein*
San Diego, California
University of Southern California

• • • • • • • •

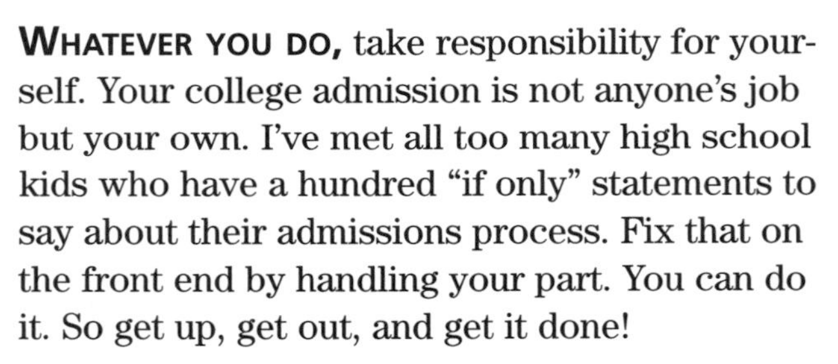

WHATEVER YOU DO, take responsibility for yourself. Your college admission is not anyone's job but your own. I've met all too many high school kids who have a hundred "if only" statements to say about their admissions process. Fix that on the front end by handling your part. You can do it. So get up, get out, and get it done!

—*Lauren Elizabeth Leahy*
Dallas, Texas
Southern Methodist University

• • • • • • • •

THE APPLICATION PROCESS was actually a lot of fun for me. I used researching and applying to schools as a sort of stress *reliever*. The stressful part for me came when I received acceptance and rejection letters. That's when the real decision came and when my list of pros and cons for schools helped a lot. My guidance counselor was invaluable as a source of information and advice. Once I finally made my decision, my mom and I had a little shopping trip and ate at my favorite restaurant to celebrate.

—*Jessica Pauley*
Chillicothe, Ohio
University of Cincinnati

PARENT TO CHILD

Some parents can be extremely overbearing, more so out of fear, since the competition to get into certain schools can be so intense. With that said, kids need to remember that their parents simply want the best for them, and that this is an overwhelming process. It helps if they can let their parents know up front, "The more you push and the more anxious you are about this, the harder it is for me." Of course, those parents may not always be willing to hear those words. This is really tricky, depending on the family dynamics.

—*Anonymous*
Palos Verdes, California

Because my parents knew they would not be playing a financial role in my college career, I refused to let them play a role in my decision about where to attend. This was difficult, because they really did not want me to attend a college that was far away, but they had no leverage to keep me close to home. Be very honest with your parents about your financial needs and your career goals. They should respect that you are serious enough to know what you need and what you want.

—*Stefanie Fry*
Knoxville, Tennessee
University of Tennessee

JUST AS WITH ANY LARGE assignment or project, I had to learn how to budget my time. My parents helped me create "due dates" for my nine college applications, and organize on a spreadsheet what I needed to get done by when. It is possible to get through, as long as you keep organized.

—*David Lichtenstein*
San Diego, California
University of Southern California

BUSINESS IS BOOMING

About 2,000 people are working full-time in the United States as private college admissions counselors.

THE FIRST TIME I WALKED INTO MY ACADEMIC adviser's office in high school, there were papers scattered all over the place and the desk was very unorganized. I realized the scope of this adviser's job and took things into my own hands. Advisers are not there to make decisions for you. They provide resources and help you find outlets to information. The best way to get a grasp on your academic planning and college entrance is to make good contacts with teachers and professors in the college you're applying to. Call up the admissions office and get the name of a student to ask a few questions. You may even find someone who is willing to show you around campus.

—*Dominic Berardi*
Cincinnati, Ohio
University of Cincinnati

KEEP MOM AND DAD AT BAY: One counselor told me that admissions offices see lots of applications that were clearly filled out by the parents and they don't like to see that. At the very least you should be able to fill out your application by yourself. Don't think that the school won't know if someone else does it for you.

—*Diane Kotchey*
Fredonia, New York
State University of New York, University at Buffalo

HEADS UP: PRIVATE COUNSELORS

In addition to the resources in your high school, you may want to get outside help in the admissions process from a private counselor. These counselors are not a replacement for your own research and work, but they can help you focus your college search and your applications.

PRO

1. A good private counselor or consultant will get to know you well and can help you figure out a personal game plan: where you should be applying, what you should do to stand out, etc.
2. They help expand your knowledge of colleges and universities and their environments.
3. They provide extra emotional support throughout the process.
4. They help you strategize about what to highlight in your essays and your applications.
5. They help manage your expectations (and Mom and Dad's) to make sure that you will be admitted somewhere that is a great fit for you.

CON

1. Private consultants are expensive.
2. They cannot "get you in," no matter what they promise. You will ultimately rise and fall on your own merits.
3. They do not have access to admissions offices. Admissions offices will speak only to your high school counselor.
4. Anyone can work as a private consultant. It's up to you to make sure you are hiring someone who is knowledgeable and experienced.
5. In the Internet age, you can do a lot of research on colleges on your own.

IF YOU FEEL THAT YOUR PARENTS are being a little too pushy and nosy about your applications, remember that they are the ones who are most likely going to be paying for college. They should be able to have as much input as they want.

—*NATHANIEL COHEN*
WEST HARTFORD, CONNECTICUT
NEW YORK UNIVERSITY

"When you start applying to colleges, it's important to learn how to delegate. Figure out what parts your parents and your counselors can help you with and ask them to do it. Never be afraid to ask for help; you don't have to do the entire thing on your own."

—*DANA NOTESTINE*
EAST POINT, GEORGIA
AGNES SCOTT COLLEGE

LISTEN TO YOUR PARENTS' and guidance counselor's input, but be honest about what you are thinking and feeling. This is your life, not theirs!

—*K. F.*
BASKING RIDGE, NEW JERSEY
LAFAYETTE UNIVERSITY

ASK THE EXPERT

If you have a connection with influence, should you use it?

Don't assume that a recommendation from the person with the fanciest title in an organization means any more than one from someone lower who actually knows you. Every year, AOs see hundreds of letters from "famous" or "important" people, but if they see that the recommenders do not know the applicants, they essentially ignore these letters. These letters only "work" when AOs understand that the person of power (who *must* have pull at the university) knows you and is really going to bat for you.

MY PARENTS WERE VERY INVOLVED, mostly by telling me what to do and what to expect. They were right about everything. My advice is to listen to your parents!

—*Mitch Royer*
Winamac, Indiana
Indiana University

ALTHOUGH I APPRECIATED the support and help my parents gave me in my college search and application process, we butted heads when they told me my first- and second-choice schools were too expensive. They didn't want me to be up to my neck in debt after graduation, and at the time I didn't understand the implications of a $47,000-a-year price tag. Today, I don't have any regrets about choosing a less expensive college. It served me well, and the program is a good fit for me.

—*Jason Torreano*
Lockport, New York
State University of New York, Brockport

ASK THE EXPERT

Don't AOs and guidance counselors work out acceptances between them?

Guidance counselors can and do call AOs to talk about students. They can help push for their students, but only so far. Ultimately, colleges will do what they want, and they keep in mind that a large portion of the applicants do not come from schools where counselors have the time or ability to make a call. They do not hold this against the students when making final decisions.

MY PARENTS WERE REALLY not involved that much. But it can work to your advantage: You have them as a resource that you can tap if you want to, but *only* if you want to. If you feel that you can handle it without their involvement, as I did, then you have that option as well. I chose to keep them at arm's length, but still within grasp if I needed them … or their checkbook!

—*BETSY LILIENTHAL*
WILMINGTON, DELAWARE
UNIVERSITY OF DELAWARE

• • • • • • • •

NEITHER OF MY PARENTS went to college and really weren't involved with the process. They did pay for all of my applications, but it was up to me to do my own research and decide where to apply. You just have to get motivated and do things on your own, because in the end, it's your choice on where you're going to spend the next four years of your life.

—*SCOTT COOLBAUGH*
KNOXVILLE, TENNESSEE
UNIVERSITY OF TENNESSEE

THE BEST RESOURCE MOST KIDS HAVE—and the one that for some reason they don't want to use—is their parents. Pick their brains as much as you can. Some kids just don't want to believe that their parents have any insight into anything. But if someone has been through the process, that person will have something to pass along. I was lucky because both of my parents are college grads. They had tons of tips for me.

—C.L.
New Middletown, Ohio
Youngstown State University

• • • • • • • •

MY PARENTS WERE VERY HELPFUL with college applications, and when we were visiting campuses. They helped me debrief after each visit: what was good, what wasn't good, how did this compare to other schools, and so on. The one thing they did that really stressed me out was to wait until late in the process to make their suggestions. If you have any opinions about where your son or daughter is going to college, state them in September, not in December.

—B.B.
Wynnewood, Pennsylvania
Brown University

• • • • • • • •

MY PARENTS HAD DEFINITE opinions about certain schools and where they thought I fit best. They were really set on Vanderbilt, which was the only school I didn't get into. I remember feeling relieved that I wouldn't have to fight them on that, and that I'd be able to go exactly where I wanted to be. Your parents want the best, but follow your heart in the college process. You're the one who has to be there for four years, not them. Make the decision yourself.

—Whitney Tritt
Atlanta, Georgia
Wake Forest University

HEADS UP: GETTING RECOMMENDATIONS

Some schools require up to three recommendations from teachers. Here are tips to make it happen.

WHOM TO ASK

- *Think about which teachers know you best.* If you sit in the back of the room and quietly earn an "A", that teacher may not have much to say about you.

- *A good recommendation* can be from someone who has watched you struggle and overcome challenges. If you come before or after school for extra help, the teacher can comment on your desire to learn and excel.

- *Consider only academic recommendations.* They should be from the English, math, science, social studies, or foreign language departments.

- *Do not worry about whether to get* recommendations from teachers who are well known. A new teacher can write a great recommendation and an experienced teacher can write a bad one.

HOW TO GET THEM

- *Request the recommendations* several weeks to a month before they are due. It is respectful of teachers' time and effort, as they will have to fill out forms for each school and spend about an hour on the recommendation itself.

- *Ask the teachers* if they want or need additional information about you, and provide that information. A good recommendation will highlight your work in class and not your broader activities, but recommenders like to know as much as they can about you.

- *Provide the recommenders* with addressed and stamped envelopes for the recommendations. They will be written and sent directly to the schools.

- *Thank your recommenders.* Write them a note and/or give them a small present. It's an acknowledgment of their effort, and that they went beyond their regular school duties.

ASK THE EXPERT

Do colleges share information about applicants?

The days when colleges shared information about you are over. Schools really only find out where else you have applied if you let them know yourself, or if you accidentally send an "I love you, Harvard" essay to Yale. Schools know you have many applications out there, and as long as you prove you are a good match, they should be happy to take you.

THE APPLICATION PROCESS was very stressful. I was trying to determine my life for the following four years, which is *not* an easy task. One major thing that helped cut back on all the stress was to use a computer that was not at my house. I always went to the counseling center to do college applications, and making the process completely separate from everything else helped me focus and get things done. I would suggest going to a library, to fill everything out and write essays.

—*Jessica*
Saratoga, California
University of Southern California

• • • • • • • •

I HAVE TWIN DAUGHTERS, and they're going to different schools by design. In the months of college applications, be prepared for some extremely stressed-out children. It's too much pressure! Get up early in the morning, fix them breakfast, and take care of some of their minor day-to-day needs, so they can concentrate just on what they need to do.

—*Lenora Wannier*
La Canada, California
P

MAKE SURE THAT THE PEOPLE INVOLVED in your application process are keeping up their end. One of my friends was so angry when he found out that he was deferred from Brown, because our high school guidance counselor had failed to send in his transcript. Fortunately, he was able to sort things out with the college and he's planning to graduate from there this year.

—*EMILY ROSE*
ATLANTA, GEORGIA
AGNES SCOTT COLLEGE

"My parents were very involved: they were picking out colleges for me! If it's too overbearing, tell them that you'll do it on your own and that you'll ask them for help when you need it."

—*LAUREN MARCINIAK*
BURR RIDGE, ILLINOIS
BRADLEY UNIVERSITY

I FELT AS IF I NEVER HAD ANY REAL GUIDANCE when I was applying. My guidance counselors were awful, and neither of my parents had gone to college, so I was pretty much on my own. I wish now that I'd been more educated; I would have gotten all those books about getting into college and read them.

—*ANONYMOUS*
DECATUR, GEORGIA
AGNES SCOTT COLLEGE

MY PARENTS HAD THE ULTIMATE say on where I went to college, because of cost and location, but I chose the schools within reasonable distance from my home. I applied on my own and knew what criteria I was looking for. Listen to your parents, but make known what you need and want in a school.

—*Adrienne Lang*
Olathe, Kansas
Texas Christian University

Work your high school teachers: They can help boost your grades. A few times, my teachers were very forgiving and rounded up!

—*Anonymous*
Toronto, Ontario
University of Toronto

ENCOURAGE YOUR CHILD TO ASK lots of questions and talk with people she knows who graduated ahead of her and who can offer their perspective on schools. We tried to speak with as many people as we could about the schools she was interested in. My daughter was introduced to two Penn alums, who wrote letters of recommendation for her. One was especially helpful in that he met with us and, after speaking with my daughter, he tried to focus on one aspect of her accomplishments that might help her stand out. He felt that her work in a political campaign was something that many high school kids would not have, so his recommendation letter to Penn emphasized that part of her background. She applied early and was accepted.

—*R.F.*
Atlanta, Georgia
P University of Pennsylvania

MY PARENTS WERE VERY INVOLVED with the process. They filled out my paperwork for me and scheduled my visits. I had to learn to be more laid back, because my mom was just as excited and controlling as I was.

—*Rachann N. McKnight*
Houston, Texas
Indiana University

ASK THE EXPERT

My recommendations are really good, don't you agree?

Do not assume you have "good" recommendations. AOs have a gut feeling about which recommendations are really sincere and which ones are not. AOs are great at understanding the nuances—like the degree to which you are really and truly respected by the person writing the letter. Choose your recommenders wisely, though, and you will be fine.

MY SON'S NOT LOOKING at what colleges have to offer in terms of education; he's looking at questions like "Can I skateboard there?" My daughter checked the University of Kentucky because it was the number one cheerleading school. I told her, "You're not going to college to cheer!" But the school was a good price and it's what she really wanted. The reality is that even though you think you know it all, parents, you haven't been to school in many years. Your kids know more than you think, and it's good practice for them. They'll soon be adults having to make decisions for themselves.

—DEBBIE
HOMEWOOD, ILLINOIS
P

MY PARENTS WERE VERY INVOLVED from the very beginning. I started looking at colleges as a high school sophomore. My parents were very enthusiastic; it didn't matter what college I chose. They were there to support me.

—JESSIE SCHOREN
LINDENWOLD, NEW JERSEY
ROWAN UNIVERSITY

THINK NEW THOUGHTS

Just because you haven't heard of a school before doesn't mean it's not the right one for you. Private counselors think of things you wouldn't have thought of. For instance, is a particular school you're interested in too rural for you? Too urban? They'll discuss interview techniques with you, how to look at schools as much as what schools to look at. They can often provide more personal attention; you can talk to them any time, not just during school hours, and can ask trivial questions. This is definitely a situation where two heads can be better than one.

THE COLLEGE SEARCH did not go without some rocky moments. My mother and I argued about possible majors, cities I could live in, financing my education—you name it. It was hard not to get frustrated. I think when you're 17 or 18 years old, the idea of doing things on your own seems incredibly appealing, and it's easy to forget just how knowledgeable your parents can be. There will be days when you and your parents will fight endlessly and days when those fights subside. Ultimately, it's important to be patient, to make the right choices for *you* and not your parents.

—*Coral A. Schneider*
Cherry Hills Village, Colorado
University of Southern California

TENSIONS WILL ARISE: Be prepared to fight with your parents. It's not exactly enjoyable, but if you know it's coming and understand it's a result of the application stress, it will be easier to handle.

—*Jessica*
Saratoga, California
University of Southern California

MY PARENTS WERE INVOLVED heavily in the decision-making process. They wanted to know what college I was interested in attending, and visited campuses with me. They stayed hands-off with the actual decision, but if your parents want to get involved, deal with it—*especially* if they are paying for it!

—*ANGELA MASSINI*
CHICAGO, ILLINOIS
BUTLER UNIVERSITY

MY PARENTS DIDN'T REALLY UNDERSTAND the complexity of the process. Their greatest gift to you would be to connect you to someone who does (or to become someone who does).

—*LAUREN ELIZABETH LEAHY*
DALLAS, TEXAS
SOUTHERN METHODIST UNIVERSITY

WHEN DECIDING WHETHER TO STAY in state or go out of state, I think most parents would prefer their kids to stay in. Mine encouraged more independence, and I think my mom was neat in that way. When I was trying to decide which way to go, my mom told me if I stayed home, my college life would just be an extension of high school. She said nothing would change, and I would always have her there to fall back on. She said if I went away, I would learn to make decisions on my own and be more independent, which is an important step in moving to adulthood.

—*JANET*
LOS ANGELES, CALIFORNIA
UNIVERSITY OF CALIFORNIA, LOS ANGELES

MY DAD IS AN ACCOUNTANT, so he handled all the student aid forms and what-not, and my mom is really good at writing résumés and essays, so she helped me out a lot. The whole process was collaborative, because my parents had my interests in mind. They let me do whatever I wanted with the process, and I usually wanted more direction from them. They even said, "You know, David, you don't have to go to college if you don't want to." To which I promptly responded, "Of course I want to go to college." But giving me the option was nice.

—DAVID BERNGARTT
CHAPEL HILL, NORTH CAROLINA
UNIVERSITY OF NORTH CAROLINA

SINCE THE COLLEGE COUNSELORS at my high school weren't very helpful, my parents enrolled me in a private counseling center. I was able to go to the center, where they had computers and snacks and counselors on hand to answer questions and edit essays. It was so helpful to take the application process away from my home. It also helped relieve a lot of stress, since the center was quiet, calm, and specifically dedicated to college admissions.

—JESSICA
SARATOGA, CALIFORNIA
UNIVERSITY OF SOUTHERN CALIFORNIA

WHAT RELIEVED MY STRESS was getting myself organized and really reflecting on where I wanted to be. I took notes on every college I visited and had files for each one. When I knew I had done everything I could possibly do, there was nothing I could stress over.

—WHITNEY TRITT
ATLANTA, GEORGIA
WAKE FOREST UNIVERSITY

YOUR SCHOOL'S COLLEGE COUNSELOR

In most high schools, a staff member is assigned to aid with the college application process. They do much more than just mail out forms: College advisers can be a valuable resource. They visit the schools, attend professional conferences, and forge relationships with the admissions staff at the colleges; they are constantly on the phone, e-mailing, and in contact with all aspects of the process, with the added advantage of insider knowledge and statistics for particular schools. Often, they are in a better position to make the right match than you would be. And they are advocating for you. Remember: You are never bugging the counselor too much!

YOUR PARENTS AREN'T TRYING to torture you; they are just thinking about your future. I think people should appreciate it when their parents put pressure on them to go to college. My dad worked really hard to get a college education. He left his family to study, and knows how much value there is in an education. The pressures he placed on me positioned me to be a better person. I think parents just want what's best for their kids.

—Anonymous
Los Angeles, California
University of California, Los Angeles

ENCOURAGE YOUR KID TO SLEEP. Have sympathy! My son was up at 6 a.m. Saturday mornings for the SAT prep class. Help your children find other outlets while going through it. Outlets can be creative and fun (like music or sports). The most important thing is to help them find balance.

—Wendy Lukehart
Takoma Park, Maryland
P

ASK FOR HELP! At first, I was very discouraged by the complexity of the entire process. Before I even delved into the land of deadlines, applications, and loans, I had to figure out where I wanted to attend. I felt stressed by the emphasis on having a reputable top five choice list, stressed by rejection letters, and stressed about making one decision that would change the course of my life. It wasn't until I asked for help that I began to be more proactive about my decision-making and more self-assured in the process. By asking one person for help, I was suddenly connected to an extensive and diverse network of schools, possibilities, counselors, and alumni.

—HEATHER MUNTZER
SANTA ROSA, CALIFORNIA
CALIFORNIA COLLEGE OF THE ARTS

• • • • • • • •

MY MOM AND DAD wanted me to find a well-rounded school, and the closer to them, the better. I just wanted to get as far away from my high school as possible. I remember my parents watching over my shoulder as I completed my applications. I needed one more to apply to, and I was out of ideas. My dad had a little sparkle in his eyes and a slight smirk as he suggested that last school. I didn't know much about it, and it was in the mid-range: not a top school, but definitely not one of the worst. I ended up going there. My university is only an hour and fifteen minutes from my parents' house, but I love it.

—K.C.
DAVIS, CALIFORNIA
UNIVERSITY OF CALIFORNIA, DAVIS

"We Are Delighted to Inform You": Acceptance (or Rejection)

All the studying, filling out of forms, writing essays, debating with your parents, visiting schools, trading stories with friends, and dreaming eventually comes down to one moment: You arrive home, or you log in to your computer, and you have mail from your top-choice school. Did you get in? Will you survive if you didn't? We asked students to relive their moments—good and bad, acceptance and rejection. Take a deep breath and read on.

THE MOMENT I GOT MY ACCEPTANCE letter, I ran outside to my parents and attempted to read it to them. After the first sentence I started crying and then went inside and danced all over my house. It was an amazing moment.

—*Jennifer Keys*
Baltimore, Maryland
New York University

BEING ACCEPTED OR BEING DECLINED IS GENERALLY A CRAPSHOOT.

—*Benjamin Berg*
Skokie, Illinois
Brandeis University

- Accept that this is a time of intense emotion.
- It may be hard to imagine, but things often work out for the best.
- Taking a gap year is a great option; Prince William did it!
- The admissions process is a learning experience.
- It seems like the end, but it's only the beginning.

IT WAS A HUGE BLOW NOT TO GET into Williams, the biggest failure I ever experienced in my life. Even though it's hard to believe at the time, things do happen for a reason. I ultimately think I would have been unhappy if I went to Williams. I don't think it was a good fit.

—*ANNE*
PITTSBURGH, PENNSYLVANIA
BROWN UNIVERSITY

NOW THEY SEND ACCEPTANCE LETTERS through e-mail. I got home from school and saw the e-mail. I read it and I screamed a lot. My parents and I were very happy.

—*HANNAH ASSADI*
SCOTTSDALE, ARIZONA
COLUMBIA COLLEGE

I DIDN'T EVEN KNOW WE HAD GOTTEN MAIL. One evening, my parents came downstairs with the video camera and a FedEx package. I opened it up. Princeton sends out a big "yes" with an exclamation point. So I saw the "Yes!" and I was just beside myself. I didn't care about anything, I was so happy. I think it was a good idea that my parents videotaped it: I would recommend it. I really want to go find that videotape and watch myself.

—*Dov Kaufmann*
Ra'anana, Israel
Princeton University

BESIDES WAITING FOR THE MAIL OR E-MAIL every day, beware the random phone call! I was notified over the phone and I was in shock. Normally you receive a big package in the mail, so you have time to stand over it, contemplate the implications of what's inside, lock yourself in a windowless room, and then slowly peel open the envelope. I had no such preparation; I just hung up on the man who called to tell me of my acceptance.

—*Nathaniel Cohen*
West Hartford, Connecticut
New York University

IF WE HAD IT TO DO OVER AGAIN, I would recommend to my son that he apply to a broader range of schools. He applied to seven schools, and while the advice is always to apply to some schools that are a "reach," some that are a "match," and some you know you'll get into, Ben pretty much reached with all of them. That meant he had to deal with rejection, which was hard.

—*Victoria Johnson*
Minneapolis, Minnesota
P Skidmore College

It was a nice sigh of relief when I got the first acceptance letter. From there, it was all downhill.

—*Scott Coolbaugh*
Knoxville, Tennessee
University of Tennessee

OTHER SIDE OF THE DESK: YOUR AO PRESENTS YOU TO THE COMMITTEE

Believe it or not, schools try to keep this process fair from the first application evaluated to the last. AOs read, evaluate, and advocate for all students equally with the same set of criteria throughout the whole process. There are systems to make sure that each application has its fair shot, and usually there is more than one reader-evaluator, especially on complicated applications and on ones that will be rejected. A few weeks before decision letters are sent, the "admitted student" statistics are evaluated and then some decisions shift according to the schools' needs: Too many students from New York? Pull a few back to the wait-list. Too few engineers for the School of Engineering? Pull a few over from the wait-list to admit. There are students who were admitted to the class but will never know it because they were yanked at the last minute to the wait-list. Those are the hardest phone calls for admissions officers to take after decisions are sent, because they really loved those students.

GETTING THE ACCEPTANCE LETTER IS, of course, the worst moment of the whole process, because your heart is beating and you cannot wait to open it. But then again, you want to wait because you're not sure what it will say.

—*Angela Massini*
Chicago, Illinois
Butler University

"When I found out I didn't get into my first-choice school, I cried, and I never cry. I feel so much better now because it was not the place for me; I think I did end up at the right school."

—*Anonymous*
Bear Creek, North Carolina
University of North Carolina at Greensboro

IT WAS THE DAY BEFORE THEY SAID it was going to be announced: Someone called me and told me that decisions were out. I was home alone except for my younger sister. I went online and typed in my password, and a big bulldog, the school mascot, popped upon the screen and said, "Welcome to the class of 2009." It was probably the happiest I had ever been in one moment. I remember a blur of jumping and yelling. I called my mom; she started crying on the phone, which was awkward because she was in a line of people at the store.

—*Zachary Klion*
Suffern, New York
Yale University

MY FIRST CHOICE WAS THE UNIVERSITY OF FLORIDA, but the school wanted a 3.6 GPA and I only had a 3.5. So I didn't make it in. I was devastated. At first, I said I wasn't going to college. But then I realized that I wanted to get out of my house and live my own life, so I applied to Florida State University. I ended up liking Florida State more than I would have liked UF. Everything happens for a reason.

—Jennifer Dragovich
Seminole, Florida
Florida State University

• • • • • • • •

THE HARDEST PART ABOUT GETTING into college was getting accepted. I had to learn to be honest on my application and not try to overachieve. After I applied, I wasn't sure how long it would take for the school to reply. I wasn't thinking about it, when I came home one night and saw a big blue envelope on the table. After I found out that I had been accepted, I began to work harder in school, not letting the fact that I was already in allow me to slack off.

—Jordyn Wilson
Greensboro, North Carolina
University of North Carolina at Greensboro

• • • • • • • •

ONCE YOU GET INTO YOUR COLLEGE, it's really amazing to hit that moment where you realize all your grades and your SAT and your APs and IBs and tests and quizzes and exams from high school are all wiped away. Once you get into college, their purpose is served, and you never have to worry about them again. Makes the whole thing seem kind of pointless (almost).

—David Berngartt
Chapel Hill, North Carolina
University of North Carolina

HARD WORK PAYS OFF

Sarah Lawrence was always my daughter Ellana's first choice, and although Ellana was wait-listed, she was very determined. She worked hard her freshman year at another school and was admitted to Sarah Lawrence for her sophomore year. Now, we both see the admissions process as being a potentially valuable coming-of-age experience. Most students and their families would never choose to spend an additional year waiting to reach last year's goal. Ellana decided to make her freshman year reflect more of her potential. She amazed us with her resolve to regroup, rethink her strategy, reapply, and eventually earn admission to Sarah Lawrence.

I was concerned about the obvious possibility that even an intensive effort might not change anything. But it did. And yet the lesson we both gained had little to do with the usual success lessons. It was worth everything because she realized she would be happy in either situation. Ellana told me that she was happy to have had a chance to work with the teachers and students she met during her freshman year. It was important to know that if she had to remain there, she would have been fine.

—*Mickie Mandel*
Riverdale, New York
P *Sarah Lawrence College*

ACCEPTANCE TIME EQUALS DECISION TIME

My dad and I had always been fans of the University of Florida. I applied for college there, as well as the University of North Carolina, which is in my home state. One day, I came home and found out by e-mail that I had gotten in to UF. My parents were going crazy. My dad and I sang the Florida fight song. Afterward, my dad made it clear that he was excited about me getting into Florida, but that he wouldn't care at all if I went to UNC instead; he'd be so happy no matter what (which was about the 100th time I'd heard that). My UNC acceptance letter kind of snuck up on me: I tore open the big envelope, fumbled around with some papers, and read the acceptance letter. Again, he flipped out. Then I called my sister, and she was super-excited. A few minutes later, after I had called everyone, my dad sat me down and said, "So, which school do you think you'd rather go to?" I told him, "UNC's at the top of my list right now." I think my dad was afraid I would think he wanted me to go to UF a lot and be influenced by that. I told him I'd still have to think about it, but per his advice, I went ahead and decided a few days later.

—*David Berngartt*
Chapel Hill, North Carolina
University of North Carolina

WHEN I GOT REJECTED, it was probably one of the worst times in my life. I got six rejections in a row. It was horrible. I'm a white male from Long Island; there wasn't anything to distinguish me. Being upset is all right, but get some perspective that this isn't the last step. The thing that got me through was knowing that this was not the end of the process. You can check out transfer programs to reassure yourself that this isn't the last go.

—*CONOR KENNEDY*
WHITESTONE, NEW YORK
BROWN UNIVERSITY

I WAS WORKING AT A RETAIL STORE at the mall and felt like I had been waiting forever for my acceptance letter to arrive. I took my 15-minute break in the middle of the afternoon, and I noticed that there were five or six phone calls from my parents. I came back to the sales floor a few minutes later, and my mom was standing there, in the middle of the store, with the big red package and a huge smile on her face. We started screaming in the middle of the mall and made absolute fools of ourselves.

—*CORAL A. SCHNEIDER*
CHERRY HILLS VILLAGE, COLORADO
UNIVERSITY OF SOUTHERN CALIFORNIA

A LONG SHOT

In 2006, Yale set an Ivy League record low in the percentage of students it admitted from its pool of applicants: just 8.6 percent of the 21,099 students who applied. Only 26 U.S. colleges—out of 2,600—accept fewer than 25 percent of applicants.

GAMING THE WAIT-LIST: DO

- *Immediately send back the form* you are offered indicating that you want to remain on the wait-list.

- *Contact the AO responsible for your application* to tell him that the school is your top choice and that you would definitely come if admitted.

- *Ask your guidance counselor to call the office* to help show that you are serious.

- *Know that this is personal*—the AO knows you and remembers you. He is human, so the more polite and sincere you are, the more you make your case.

- *Try to assess if there are any weaknesses you can address.* Usually there is nothing to do at this point, but ask what the AO would like to see.

GAMING THE WAIT-LIST: DON'T

- *Call when you are crying or angry.* Make your reasoned case yourself (your parent should not call!) it will be noted in your application, and you should be put on a shorter list.

- *Become a pain.* E-mailing or calling daily may look like a good plan, but attacking the AO and sending in extra information every day can become annoying and cause the AO to dislike you instead of wanting to be your advocate. Send letters and make phone calls, but be judicious.

- *Do nothing.* Schools will only offer admission to interested students (they want 100 percent yield from the wait-list) so they will not extend offers to students who have not continued to express interest.

- *Forget that often this is not about you*, but about internal admissions needs. Schools wait-list for a number of statistical reasons, and there are applicants AOs love that they will be dying to take from the wait-list later, if they are able to. Your phone call can help assess this.

I FOUND OUT BY E-MAIL. They tell you to check your e-mail at 8 o'clock. I checked and it wasn't there, so I got into the shower, and my little sister went onto my computer and the e-mail had come in. She clicked on it, it opened, and she saw what it was. Right away, she clicked the "minimize" button and ran out of the room. I came back to the computer and was trying to figure out why the screen looked different than when I left it. Then my sister tiptoed in and said, "I think you got your e-mail." So I made everybody leave the room, I shut all the doors and I gave myself a moment to meditate. I opened the e-mail and the first thing I saw was, "We are delighted to inform you …" I was pretty ecstatic. Then I screamed and told my family. Everybody was screaming and shrieking and I thought the house was going to fall down.

—Dana
Lawrence, New York
Harvard University

Contrary to popular belief, it is my experience that a "Yes!" can come as easily in a small envelope as in a big manila one.

—April
Chicago, Illinois
Purdue University

I APPLIED FOR EARLY DECISION. I got deferred, and then I applied to seven other schools. I eventually made my first choice: Brown. After the application was deferred, I applied by regular admission. I wrote the admissions office a letter saying Brown was still my first choice. I think that follow-up letter was really important. I had done some interesting things since I had first applied to school. I also had more grades. Anything you can do to help yourself stand out is good.

—B.B.
Wynnewood, Pennsylvania
Brown University

PUBLIC MEANS PUBLIC

Watch out when contributing to Web sites that discuss colleges. AOs visit those sites, too, to read students' comments and impressions about schools. Sometimes AOs can actually figure out who you are. Do not call AOs "adcoms" (a strange new word developed by students from "admissions" and "committee") or profess to know how they think—admissions officers are professionals and individuals.

Don't take advice from students on any of these sites about "chances for admission." Professionals in the field cannot—and should not—predict your chances with accuracy, so random students, who know nothing more than your statistics, certainly cannot predict your chances. These forums are full of misinformation about the application process, the committee processes, games to play, and schools' weaknesses. If you have questions, go to the AO directly!

In addition, be aware of what you say about yourself on *MySpace.com*, or on similar social or school Web sites. Your comments might be read by those considering you for admission; it's happened before. Make sure you show only your best self to the public.

HEADS UP: ON TRANSFERRING

You've already heard that you should apply only to schools you'd want to attend. If you're now looking at your acceptances and thinking, "I can always transfer," you're right—but there's a catch. Transferring, from a social point of view, is not a lot of fun.

- Many friendships are forged in freshman year.
- You might get the worst choice in dorms.
- Your course credits may not transfer.
- You have to be more assertive to assimilate.
- You bond more with the college in your first year.
- Your freshman year is the most exciting, when everything is new and no one knows anyone else.

So, do your best to make your first choice the right one!

WHEN I HEARD I GOT IN, I ran out of the admissions office. My mom and I were going crazy. I called my dad and then my boyfriend. I went to my high school theater teacher, who had been helping me. Later, we went out to dinner. We had Chinese food, my favorite takeout.

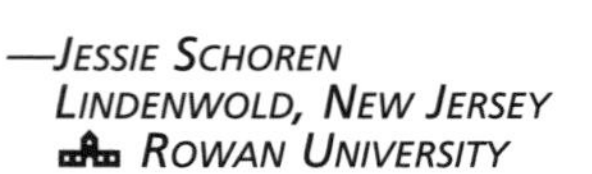

—*JESSIE SCHOREN*
LINDENWOLD, NEW JERSEY
ROWAN UNIVERSITY

ONE THING THAT YOU MIGHT NOT HEAR from your parents but is important to know: Do not *freak out* if you don't get into your college of choice. Sure, there might be some school that fits perfectly into your life's grand scheme, but odds are, you're not even gonna stick with whatever plan you have right now. The most important thing about college is college! It's about going off on your own, meeting new people, getting involved, being responsible for yourself. Whether you go to State or Tech or A&M or whatever, you're going to learn a lot both in and out of the classroom. All the rankings and name recognition of schools sometimes gets people's heads in a spin about which school is a "good" school and which school is not. But college is what you make of it. You should be excited about getting out there on your own, no matter where you're going.

—*DAVID BERNGARTT*
CHAPEL HILL, NORTH CAROLINA
UNIVERSITY OF NORTH CAROLINA

WHEN OUR SON FINALLY got the acceptance from Skidmore, that was the perfect moment.

—*VICTORIA JOHNSON*
MINNEAPOLIS, MINNESOTA
P SKIDMORE COLLEGE

WHAT HAPPENED TO A SAFETY AND A REACH?

It is not unheard of for today's students to apply to 20 or more colleges ... and get accepted to every single one.

I got turned down from five colleges before I found one that would have me. Hey, it happens to the best of us!

—*Trina Cooke*
Struthers, Ohio

If you don't get accepted at first, don't waste any time crying. I wasn't accepted the first time I applied to UCLA. When I first received the bad news, I went into hibernation. Then I realized that everything happens for a reason, and there was no point in crying over something I had no control over. Plus, by staying in my room, I was missing out on other things in life.

—*Anonymous*
Los Angeles, California
University of California, Los Angeles

Because my grades were so-so, Purdue sent me a "Get grades of B's or better this semester and we'll let you in" letter. Apparently, all I needed was a little motivation to get my grades up. I was really excited and proud of myself once I got the acceptance letter, partially because I wanted to go, but mostly because I wasn't sure what I would do if I didn't get in.

—*April*
Chicago, Illinois
Purdue University

The director of admissions actually called me to say that all my references were in, and she said that my chances looked good. It was several years before I realized how amazing that phone call was—didn't everyone get that phone call? When I got the letter, I did that whole thing about "Oh, it's a thick letter—that's good news." But then I thought, well, maybe they just had a lot of bad things to say. I was frozen for a minute or two. I was so overwhelmed at what I'd gotten myself into.

—*Nancy Poehlmann*
Atlanta, Georgia
Agnes Scott College

A FEW WORDS ON REJECTION

- Rejection is not personal: You are still a worthwhile person.
- Getting into colleges will continue to be difficult for the next several years simply because of the population—it's a seller's market right now.
- Even the top schools turn away a certain percentage of the valedictorians and salutatorians who apply each year. William Fitzsimmons, Dean of Admissions at Harvard College, has admitted that probably 80 percent of the students who apply there would be admissible; the problem is, they simply can't take that many.
- If you are rejected by every school you applied to, fear not: Counselors receive a list of schools that are still accepting students in April. And sometimes they can even get students into a school that has officially stopped accepting applicants.

THE ACCEPTANCE LETTER CAME two days late, so naturally I was at the edge of my very uncomfortable seat for two long days. Once it came, though, everything fell into place. I realized that it wasn't just one grade or one SAT score or what I did every day after school or even how many community service hours I had. It was the whole package they were looking for, and it was an incredible moment to read that they had "chosen me to join the class of 2009." At that moment, all of your hard work is commended, and you should feel great about what you have just achieved.

—Jackie Adlam
Mill Valley, California
Colgate University

MY SON DID NOT GET INTO HIS FIRST OR SECOND choice of schools. He was very upset. Rather than let him attend his "safety" school, which he was not at all excited about, I encouraged him to take a year off and do something meaningful. He ended up finding a program called National Outdoor Leadership School (NOLS) and was accepted into its Semester in the Rockies. He is studying under the big sky and stars of Wyoming, Utah, and Colorado for the whole fall semester and is earning 16 college credits. He plans to reapply to college this January for next fall.

—Lisa
Poughkeepsie, New York
P

Decision Tree: Picking the Right School

Congratulations! You got into college! Actually, several colleges. Now you've got to choose the place you want to spend at least four years of your life; set the success standard for your pending career; meet that special someone or lifelong friend. The good news is that the decision is up to you; the bad news is that it's up to you! Read on to discover how others made their final choices.

BE TRUE TO YOURSELF ABOUT what you want to get out of school. Don't fool yourself about being someone you're not. Don't base your choice on what other people are doing.

—*BETH MAYEROWITZ*
NEW YORK, NEW YORK
UNIVERSITY OF WISCONSIN

DO YOU WANT TO GO TO A SCHOOL WHERE YOU KNOW PEOPLE OR WHERE YOU'LL START TOTALLY FRESH?

—*JOSH TIZEL*
TORONTO, ONTARIO
YORK UNIVERSITY

- Spend some quality alone-time, thinking about what you really want.
- Weigh all the factors: distance, cost, size, curriculum, climate, atmosphere.
- Yes, it can be stressful, but everyone else is going through it too.
- No double-depositing—make a grownup choice and stick to it.
- Its how you spend your time in college, more than the school itself, that shapes your future.

I THOUGHT I KNEW EXACTLY where I wanted to go, what I wanted to major in, all the little details. But once I got accepted and had to make a choice, I was a wreck, knowing that this would be one of the biggest decisions of my life. Spend some time alone thinking about what *you* want, not what your friends or parents want.

—*Sheila Crawford*
Cary, North Carolina
North Carolina State Universiry

I'M ORIGINALLY FROM TEXAS and I just wanted to get out for a while. I hadn't been to Colorado before, so that's where I decided to go.

—*Trent*
Grapevine, Texas
University of Colorado

THE EARLIER YOU CHOOSE A SCHOOL, the more options you have open to you when you try to find a place to live. I waited until almost the last minute to submit my application. Once I finally received my acceptance letter, I had to find an apartment, a job, pack, and move in about three weeks' time. It was a lot of unnecessary stress that easily could have been avoided!

—Ashley Yow
San Antonio, Texas
Texas State University

"I went on the Web sites of schools and found out where the hottest girls were! Nah, that's not true: I wanted to be in a diverse city and my school was in a great area, so that's why I applied to York!"

—Josh Tizel
Toronto, Ontario
York University

KNOWING WHAT YOU'RE GOING TO BE "when you grow up" should factor into your decision of which school to attend. I wanted to be a veterinarian, so I chose a college that has a vet school. This school has pre-vet in undergrad, so I took biomedical science and started working towards this career.

—Jill
Toronto, Ontario

REMEMBER THAT YOU'RE THE ONLY PERSON who knows yourself and what you want. The other day, I told my brother, who is applying to college, that he is the only one who knows what he wants. He's getting a lot of information from everyone, including me, and he should filter it. Ultimately, he's the one making the decision.

—*Anastasia*
Baltimore, Maryland
Yale University

Easy decision: I went to school where my older sister went to school!

—*Janna Harowitz*
Vancouver, British Columbia
McGill University

BE ABSOLUTELY SURE IT'S WHERE you want to go. It's a hard decision to take back. The first college I went to, Ithaca, there were too many pressures. It was too far away. It didn't have a major I could live with. Now I'm transferring to Rutgers next year. It's kind of absurd.

—*William Alvarez*
Lyndhurst, New Jersey
Rutgers University

I KNEW THAT UNC WOULD BE ABLE to offer both academics and a lively social scene—the balance was important to me.

—*Jillian Nadell*
Greensboro, North Carolina
University of North Carolina

I WAS ACCEPTED TO DEPAUL, Tennessee, and Houston. I decided on Tennessee because it was in a completely new place where I didn't know anybody. Houston was a little too far away and DePaul was very expensive, especially since it's in Chicago. I liked Knoxville and how it's centered around the campus.

—*Scott Coolbaugh*
Knoxville, Tennessee
University of Tennessee

PARENT TO PARENT

OUR DAUGHTER THOUGHT FROM THE BEGINNING that she wanted a big school in a reasonably big city, but there was a smaller school in Portland, Oregon, that she was interested in. She was accepted and flew out there from Minneapolis by herself, visited the college on her own, and stayed in a dorm. It was an expensive trip, but I'm glad she went because she realized that even though she really liked Portland, the school wasn't big enough to sustain her for four years. She realized that she was right all along: that she wanted to go to a big school because of all the things it could offer. She ended up at the University of Michigan and has been very happy there.

—M.B.
MINNEAPOLIS, MINNESOTA
P UNIVERSITY OF MICHIGAN

• • • • • • • •

LOOK VERY CAREFULLY AT ANY PARTICULAR NEEDS your children might have. If they're reluctant to go to school or lack independence, consider all of that in choosing a school, whether it's large, small, close to home. Don't lock yourself in to thinking it has to be four years of nothing but school. You can consider combining work and school. I think the most important thing to impress upon children going to school is that there's no single way to do it. Don't try to rush it if it needs to be taken slowly.

—CINDY
HERNDON, VIRGINIA
P GEORGE MASON UNIVERSITY

WE LIKE YOU, BUT ...

I applied to the University of Chicago and Brown. I got an acceptance to the University of Chicago in the fall, but became less enthused about it once I got in. Then Brown did this incredibly weird thing: it admitted me the year after my class, which I've never heard of, but it exists. The school sent me a letter in July that said, "Look, we admitted you in the class for the year behind you." That was kind of shocking, especially since it was in an envelope that said, "Congratulations!" The condition was that I couldn't matriculate anywhere else and I couldn't take classes at Brown even as a shadowy semi-student. I just had to *not* be in college for a year. So I went to the University of Chicago.

—Bobby
Maplewood, New Jersey
University of Chicago

I DECIDED TO PURSUE DANCE ON A COLLEGE LEVEL. I needed to make a résumé, get head shots taken, take pictures of myself in various dance poses, choreograph solos, and describe my goals and where I saw myself as a dancer after I had graduated from the school. I remember feeling completely overwhelmed by everything. Not only did I apply to schools the same way everyone else did; I had to fly to several cities around the country for auditions. I had to understand that there are tons of options for a career and that dance is not necessarily the "safe" road to travel. Still, I made a conscious decision to pursue something I loved.

—Jennifer Keys
Baltimore, Maryland
New York University

I APPLIED AND GOT ACCEPTED to so many schools that the final decision killed me. I can't tell you how many times I walked out to my mailbox ready to send my letter of intent to my chosen school, only to bring it right back in the house to change my mind. I think I practiced this ritual at least five times during the few weeks I had to make my final decision.

—Janet
Los Angeles, California
University of California, Los Angeles

"Think really carefully about what size you want your college to be. I only looked at schools of 1,500 or less, and that ended up being smaller than I realized. You can get tired of seeing the same faces pretty quickly."

—Kayleigh Shebs
Ambridge, Pennsylvania
Agnes Scott College

I HAD TO CHOOSE BETWEEN Rutgers University and NYU. Because Rutgers and NYU were the same-caliber schools, my parents and I chose Rutgers because it was more affordable. But if I had to do it over, I would have attended NYU. I love New York City!

—Lisa Greenbaum
New York, New York
Rutgers University

LEARNING EXPERIENCE: DEALING WITH STRESS

TO AVOID STRESS, SET CERTAIN TIMES OF EACH DAY to worry about admissions, and during the rest of the time, try not to deal with it. Go out with friends, go to the movies, go tip a cow ... anything but worrying about school.

—K.R.
WINCHESTER, VIRGINIA
UNIVERSITY OF VIRGINIA

• • • • • • • •

THE PROCESS WAS STRESSFUL BECAUSE, in addition to filling out applications, I had to deal with the busyness of senior year activities, including playing a varsity sport the fall of my senior year. To lessen the stress, I started filling out my applications as soon as they were released so I didn't have to complete them all at once. Looking back, I wish that I had taken a day or two off from school to work solely on my applications and get them out of the way.

—CARRIE BERTOLOZZI
CHAPEL HILL, NORTH CAROLINA
UNIVERSITY OF NORTH CAROLINA

• • • • • • • •

THE COLLEGE APPLICATION PROCESS OFTEN EXAGGERATES the actual importance of where you go to college. More important than *where* you go to college is whether you excel when you are there. In other words, a high average at an average school is almost always better then an *average* average at a great school. Always keep that in mind.

—NATHANIEL COHEN
WEST HARTFORD, CONNECTICUT
NEW YORK UNIVERSITY

• • • • • • • •

I TRIED TO LESSEN THE STRESS BY STAYING INVOLVED in my high school activities such as volleyball, tennis, theater, and volunteering.

—STEFANIE FRY
KNOXVILLE, TENNESSEE
UNIVERSITY OF TENNESSEE

BEING A RECRUITED ATHLETE IS TOUGH. You're trying to take care of the recruiting trips while not letting your grades slip in high school. But it's only as stressful as you let it become. I had to cut things out. I had to skip a couple of practices during the school year. You can't do everything. You can't keep all the plates spinning.

—MATTHEW BAKER
SILVER SPRINGS, MARYLAND
YALE UNIVERSITY

• • • • • • • •

THE WAY I BLEW OFF STEAM IN RELATION to the college application experience was to ignore it. That was not in my best interest. I essentially decided that I shouldn't think about it a whole lot and just applied to three schools with this nihilistic attitude, like, "Wherever I get in, I'm going." Yes, there is some parity among colleges. But you should spend more time choosing your school than I did.

—BOBBY
MAPLEWOOD, NEW JERSEY
UNIVERSITY OF CHICAGO

• • • • • • • •

IT WAS VERY STRESSFUL TO WAIT TO HEAR FROM SCHOOLS, thinking about the uncertainty of where I was going to be the next year. Also, knowing I was competing with my friends proved to be stressful when the results came in, especially when I got accepted in places they didn't. I thought the stress would end after we got the acceptance letters back, but it didn't. It's helpful that most people around you are going through the same thing, so you're stressing together.

—B.B.
WYNNEWOOD, PENNSYLVANIA
BROWN UNIVERSITY

MAKE SURE THAT YOU RESEARCH YOUR MAJOR and your potential career path. You want to go to a school that offers both the curriculum and the experience that you are looking for. Ask the school about student life, and if you can speak with some students and visit some student groups. Also, get an outline of the courses that you will be taking; it's important that the major you want has a wide variety of courses to take.

—ANDREW J. BURKE
CINCINNATI, OHIO
UNIVERSITY OF CINCINNATI

MY UNIVERSITY IS A VERY LAID-BACK and friendly school. It's easy to fit in with people and its not too challenging academically. But it is three girls to one guy, so it isn't optimal for dating. You should look at the ratios when you're applying if you're interested in meeting someone!

—JILL
TORONTO, ONTARIO

KEEP IN MIND THAT THERE will always be trade-offs to any experience. Sometimes I wish I'd gone to a bigger school with more options for my major, but then I'd probably lose the sense of community I have here.

—ELIZABETH SATTIN
ATLANTA, GEORGIA
AGNES SCOTT COLLEGE

RED OR BLUE?

Hillsdale College in Hillsdale, Michigan, was recently ranked America's most conservative college. Mills College in Oakland, California, was ranked the most liberal.

IT WAS REALLY IMPORTANT FOR ME to choose a school with an active Jewish community so that I wouldn't have to deal with finding my niche religiously, knowing that college is a tough transition anyway. I was also struggling with going to a huge school after going to a small private school for my whole life, but I've found that wherever you go to school, big or small, a person will be faced with this challenge.

—*Elana Brownstein*
Baltimore, Maryland
University of Maryland, College Park

• • • • • • • •

I GOT THE LIST DOWN TO MY TWO top choices—Marquette and Illinois Wesleyan—and sat down to figure out the pros and cons of each. Wesleyan is a pretty small school. About 60 people from my high school were going there, and I didn't want to run into them every day. Marquette is in a city, so there's always something to do, but it's small enough that it's easy to get around. It also has a broadcast program, which I wanted, the campus and dorms were nice, and my mom was in love in with the school. And only two other people from my high school were going there.

—*Ashley Little*
Flossmoor, Illinois
Marquette University

• • • • • • • •

I TRIED TO FIND A GOOD BALANCE. My school had to have a great program in the subject I wanted to study, could not be too big so that I could get more personal attention if I needed it, was located far enough from my parents, and also fun for me to discover on my own.

—*Stephen Mackay*
South Orange, New Jersey
University of California, Riverside

SOMETIMES FINANCES HELP YOU DECIDE. I originally applied to Seton Hall because it was in New Jersey, and I was accepted. But when the bill came, it was obvious I couldn't afford it. I took a year off and applied to state schools that I could afford. My sister was dating some guy who went to Rowan, so I went with her to check it out and liked it. It was affordable, and the school accepted me.

—*JAMIE HARGRAVE*
NUTLEY, NEW JERSEY
ROWAN UNIVERSITY

Go for environment; go to a school in a place where you'd go to visit.

—*IAIN BURNETT*
REDWOOD CITY, CALIFORNIA
UNIVERSITY OF CALIFORNIA, SANTA BARBARA

I APPLIED TO UCLA, UC BERKELEY, AND UCI. UCLA and UCI were particularly appealing at the time, because they were close to home. But I definitely do not recommend this! Living at home may seem like a comfortable, financially sound idea; but it also may be developmentally stunting, and I think moving away is a big step toward independence. That's why I chose Berkeley. It's so different from what I was used to (Orange County), and that's a good thing. I felt I could learn a lot more here outside of the textbooks and problems I would have to plow through. I was right.

—*TRICIA POWELL*
HUNTINGTON BEACH, CALIFORNIA
UNIVERSITY OF CALIFORNIA, BERKELEY

I WAS RECRUITED BY A NUMBER OF SCHOOLS in my state and out of state, but I only applied to one and got in. The reason for my selection: This school was five blocks from my house, and none of the other schools were willing to move their campuses down the block from me.

—*LINDSEY MORRISON GRANT*
PORTLAND, OREGON
CONCORDIA UNIVERSITY, PORTLAND

I BASED MY DECISION ON THE TWO FACTORS that, in hindsight, are probably *least* important: cost and location. If you are going to make the huge commitment of going to college, you shouldn't worry about those things. They are minor details.

—*BRENDA PENDLETON*
NEWARK, DELAWARE
UNIVERSITY OF DELAWARE

"My dad wanted me to settle for a school. Don't settle unless you have to. It's your education, so be assertive. If you know you want a school near the ocean and you live in the Midwest, push for the ocean. Otherwise, you're not going to be happy."

—*KATHRYN*
PHILADELPHIA, PENNSYLVANIA
SARAH LAWRENCE COLLEGE

IT MAY SEEM SILLY when you're applying for college to think of college graduation, but I wish I'd had that mind-set. If you go to school in a small town, for example, you may not get big firms from New York heading your way to recruit.

—*AMANDA NELSON*
NEW YORK, NEW YORK
UNIVERSITY OF WISCONSIN

OTHER SIDE OF THE DESK: THE JOB'S NOT OVER

Decisions are out, and now you will see the marketing machine back in action. AOs and current students, as well as the academic areas of the college, will be in touch to show you the reasons you should attend their college, and the schools run visiting programs to work on yield. A little secret: AOs often remember you, your story, and your application details well, but when you visit, the receptionist will let the AO know you are there and the AO sometimes quickly brushes up on you by looking at his notes in your application. It is a bit of a game, but it is also a way to have the most informed conversation possible with you.

BE REALISTIC. If you are not the most studious person, don't go to an extremely rigorous school. At the same time, if you have enough potential in your chosen field, opt for a school that will help you to be the best you can be in your field. And absolutely do not base your decision on location!

—*Courtney Heilman*
Boston, Massachusetts

BE SELECTIVE DURING THE APPLICATION PROCESS. My parents told me to do as much as I could do to narrow my choices so I could focus attention on fewer schools. They said that when you get in, you'll know it's where you want to go. Try to avoid getting into 20 schools. Other people applying to college might get screwed if you apply to a school you don't even want to go to and you get accepted and take their place.

—*Brian Rosen*
New York, New York
Princeton University

MY PARENTS HAD SOME STRINGENT IDEAS on which schools were the best for me. I got them to consider other schools by doing research and selling them on things like low student-teacher ratio, the percentage of high SATs, and the like. If you're trying to convince your parents to let you go to a school other than the one they prefer, I recommend this tactic: Sell, sell, sell!

—Nancy Poehlmann
Atlanta, Georgia
Agnes Scott College

THE FIRST THING, OTHER THAN MONEY, that you should worry about is which school is best in the field that you want to get into. I want to get into early childhood education, and my school is one of the best schools in the area for that. Plus, it is very advanced technologically, with the whole campus now wireless. It's good to keep those kinds of amenities in mind.

—Rachel Lynch
Frederick, Maryland
Coppin State University

I WAS NERVOUS THAT I KNEW TOO MANY PEOPLE at Maryland. It's my state school and a very popular choice for people from my high school, so I was afraid I wouldn't meet new people. I was so wrong. I have stayed close with some of my friends from high school who are in college with me, but I've met tons of amazing new people in college, through social activities, classes, and even through friends from high school. It has also been nice to see familiar faces when walking around campus.

—Elana Brownstein
Baltimore, Maryland
University of Maryland, College Park

Pick a school that is not beyond your abilities. Getting good grades from good schools rather than poor grades from a top-tier school puts you in good standing for the future.

—J.K.D.
Pittsburgh, Pennsylvania
P Kent State University

OTHER SIDE OF THE DESK: JUST DON'T DO IT

Playing games with colleges is unethical. Period. Sending in a deposit and your signature reserving your place in the class is a commitment (even if it is not legally binding) and you are expected to honor it. Putting down a deposit at two or more schools is not allowed, and if colleges find out, *both* schools will rescind your admission out of respect for each other. Colleges play fair with each other and will not fight for you if you do this. College deans are long-time respected colleagues and friends.

To withdraw because you have been accepted off the wait-list at another school, or because an unforeseen major family crisis has occurred, is fine. To withdraw because you simply want a different school is unethical. Schools do plan for a "summer melt"—a certain number of students who will ultimately withdraw—but to fool around with deposits takes away the opportunity for students who really want to be at these schools. Also, you are becoming an adult, responsible for making decisions. It is not ethical to double-deposit just because you simply cannot make up your mind. Grow up and decide.

I ULTIMATELY CHOSE PURDUE BECAUSE, in my opinion, it has the best reputation of all of the public schools in Indiana. Of course, I was sticking with an in-state public school to save on cash. Some of my friends have major debt from school.

—APRIL
CHICAGO, ILLINOIS
PURDUE UNIVERSITY

• • • • • • • •

I WAS RECRUITED AS A FOOTBALL PLAYER. When it came down to it, I had to choose between Yale, Harvard, Brown, and a few other places. Even though you're going to be a student-athlete, you're going to be spending the majority of your time in your room or with friends going out to eat. You spend time with people in your dorm and in classes. Go to classes and stay with a student. Visit everywhere on campus to help you make your decision.

—MATTHEW BAKER
SILVER SPRINGS, MARYLAND
YALE UNIVERSITY

• • • • • • • •

COLUMBIA JUST FELT RIGHT. I just like the general feeling of coming here. It felt like I would belong.

—HANNAH ASSADI
SCOTTSDALE, ARIZONA
COLUMBIA COLLEGE

TRI-STATE = THREE TIMES THE PARTIES!

Tri-State University in Angola, Indiana, is ranked America's top party school—42 percent of surveyed Tri-State students said they party three to five nights per week.

HEADS UP: COMPARING OFFERS AND PACKAGES

With acceptance at several schools that you adore, how can you compare your options? Think about these factors in making your decision:

- Where do you feel the most comfortable?
- How much of a financial burden will this put on your family—does it go too far?
- Is it worth the free ride at a place you hate, or a financial investment in a great match?

OTHER SCHOOLS SENT ME A FORM acceptance letter, but Oakland sent me holiday cards when I got in. In November they sent me a Thanksgiving card, then holiday and New Year's cards, personally written by someone in the admissions office. I liked that. It made me feel really special. Before, I thought I was a mediocre student. With the cards, I felt like someone wanted me.

—*MINEHAHA FORMAN*
SAN ANTONIO VILLAGE, BELIZE
OAKLAND UNIVERSITY

THE MOST SIGNIFICANT ADVICE I gave my son was that no school would make him happy, smart, or successful. His choices are what will do that. Therefore, what school he got into was not that big of a deal.

—*BETH REINGOLD GLUCK*
ATLANTA, GEORGIA
P UNIVERSITY OF SOUTHERN CALIFORNIA

ASK FOR ADVICE. There was a guy I knew who was a great actor who recommended the Theatre Program at the University of Toronto, so I trusted his suggestion.

—*MICHAEL ALBERT PAOLI*
TORONTO, ONTARIO
UNIVERSITY OF TORONTO

• • • • • • • •

I KNEW I WANTED TO APPLY to engineering schools, so I first picked out the best one that was free (in-state), which was Georgia Tech. I then picked the one that was the most highly regarded, which was Berkeley. Finally, just to have a third option, and on the advice of a neighbor, I added a third that my neighbor's daughter had attended, which was Purdue.

—*P.T.*
ATLANTA, GEORGIA
PURDUE UNIVERSITY

• • • • • • • •

ACADEMICS ARE IMPORTANT, but I considered the whole picture when I was making my decision. While I needed a place to grow academically, I would also be growing socially, physically, emotionally, and spiritually. Determine what your values are, and find an institution that complements your values.

—*DAVID*
MUNCIE, INDIANA
ANDERSON UNIVERSITY

PEER TO PEER

Most college and university Web sites lack a sense of the real student life that goes on there. One way to catch that flavor is to check out the Web section that's meant for current students, for a sense of day-to-day campus life.

MAKE SURE YOU LOOK AT A LOT OF different kinds of schools, liberal arts and technical, before you apply. I picked a small liberal arts school, but I majored in science. I would probably have been better off in a more technical program.

—A.M.
DECATUR, GEORGIA
AGNES SCOTT COLLEGE

I DECIDED TO GO TO SCHOOL IN MY HOMETOWN because my plan was to go abroad for a year, and I felt that if I was going away from home, I could be in my hometown for the other years of school. I ended up spending my third year overseas, and it was a great experience.

—SHIRA
TORONTO, ONTARIO
YORK UNIVERSITY

THE CRITERIA YOU'LL USE AS PARENTS may look different than those of your kids. My son is thinking of attending the University of Washington. I have a feeling it's because he has a girlfriend going to school in Seattle.

—RICH HEIDORN
SILVER SPRING, MARYLAND
P

SAY YES TO CHAT

Online chat sessions are often scheduled on college Web sites near acceptance deadlines. These sessions provide a good opportunity to ask honest questions and get straight answers. And if you receive a phone call from a student representative, take the call and advantage of the opportunity; ask about everything you want to know.

FOLLOW YOUR HEART

Ever since I was old enough to start thinking about college, I had thought that I would go to North Central College, a tiny liberal arts school in Naperville, Illinois. My parents were alumni of the school, as was my cousin. My parents both majored in business, and several years after they graduated, they were married in the college's chapel. Needless to say, the school meant a lot to them. So when I began visiting schools my junior year, North Central was still at the top of my list. My parents would tell me the great times they had there, which of course made the school more desirable. However, I still wanted to see what was out there. It wasn't until I visited Bradley that I knew I had a tough decision to make. I immediately fell in love with the campus and could even picture myself there. All along, my parents would still tell me how great North Central was, but they never pressured me or made me feel like I had go there. I competed in a scholarship competition at North Central and received a nice amount of money; it was then that I had to make my final decision. Do I accept the award and follow in my parents' footsteps as they hoped? Or do I follow my heart and go where I felt I would be extremely happy? After much discussion, I realized that I needed to have my own college experience and memories. I decided I would attend Bradley. College is when you grow the most as a person. Having an experience like no other is something you will carry with you for the remainder of your life.

—*Laura*
Tinley Park, Illinois
Bradley University

CHARTING YOUR COURSE

If you are having trouble deciding between two or more schools (lucky you!), try this method:

Make a chart, listing each school along the left, vertical (Y) axis, and the following attributes along the top, horizontal (X) axis:

- Location
- Climate
- Majors
- Class sizes
- Extracurriculars
- Make-up of students

Add a column for any other attribute you want to evaluate.

For each school, assign a value from 1–5 to each attribute, where 1 is the least favorable, 3 is neutral, and 5 is the most favorable.

When all the boxes are filled in, total the points for each school: You may have a winner.

Open Your Mind: Imagining the College Life

So, what is it like, really? We're talking about college. Do the leaves turn gold and blanket the quad with an ethereal sheen? Do the students and professors sip espresso and talk about the keys to the universe? Do the dorms feature a continuous soundtrack by Simon & Garfunkel? Or is college more like a Nelly video mixed with a raucous college movie comedy? Should you really expect that much beer and sex? No matter what you picture, the reality is probably different. Read on for a head start on the college life.

AS A HIGH SCHOOL SENIOR, I pictured college people acting much more mature. It's taken me a few years to realize that people don't really change from high school. They just get older and do stupider things!

—*MICHAEL ABRAMOVITZ*
TUCSON, ARIZONA
UNIVERSITY OF ARIZONA

I DON'T THINK THAT ANYONE IS TRULY "READY" FOR ANYTHING, SO JUMP IN, AND TRUST YOURSELF.

—*BRIANA*
SONOMA, CALIFORNIA
SONOMA STATE UNIVERSITY

- Surprise! People are the same everywhere.
- Remember, with freedom comes responsibility.
- Prepare to be pushed *and* prepare to push yourself.
- Don't fall for senioritis—those final grades do count!
- Imagine yourself in four years' time, then decide what to do to become that person.

I IMAGINED THAT COLLEGE STUDENTS studied all night. Once I was there, I found that through proper time management, I had more study/social life balance than I anticipated. Plus, I didn't do as perfectly as I imagined I would.

—*William Watts*
Berkeley, California
University of California, Berkeley

I IMAGINED COLLEGE STUDENTS to be serious and snobby and generally to take themselves too seriously. I expected a lot of pretension. I did find that at school, but I also found a group of friends that I will have for the rest of my life.

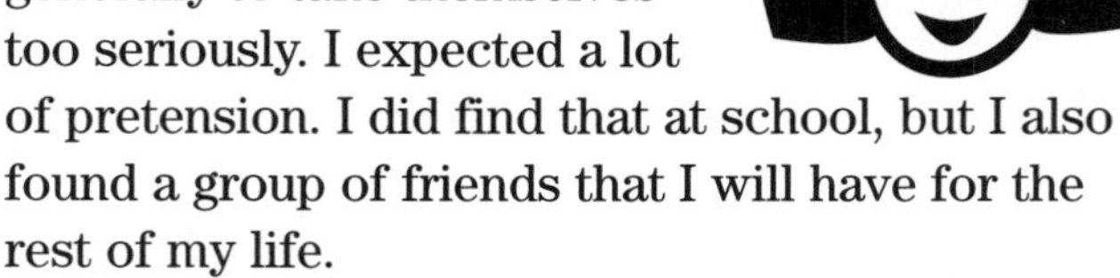

—*Michael Albert Paoli*
Toronto, Ontario
University of Toronto

I THOUGHT SCHOOL WOULD BE TOUGH and that I would have to work much harder than I did in high school. Turned out, it wasn't as demanding as I had imagined. I was pretty independent to begin with, so living on my own wasn't such a big deal.

—*JAMIE HARGRAVE*
NUTLEY, NEW JERSEY
ROWAN UNIVERSITY

"You find the same people in college you find everywhere else. Bottom line: You find what you're looking for. Keep an open attitude and you'll be fine."

—*ERIN*
TACOMA, WASHINGTON

I WAS EXCITED TO GET AWAY FROM HOME and to experience the party life of school that I had heard so much about. To me, these things seemed very "college." Another thing I expected to get out of my college experience was the education! Shocking, I know, but I did enjoy the access to more sophisticated courses and the encouragement you're given in college to talk about real issues. In high school you can't delve as much into these things, so I was excited to explore different topics and be on my own. I saw college as a chance to grow up.

—*JILL*
TORONTO, ONTARIO

THIS IS YOUR BRAIN INCOLLEGE

I imagined the life of a college student to be full of freedom with lots of partying and not too many responsibilities. I was only half right. I did have freedom, but I also had the responsibility of taking care of myself. The hardest thing about college was getting up to go to class. When I didn't, I didn't do so hot. When I did, I did pretty well. It's pretty sobering to know that to do well, all you have to do is go to class and do a little work outside of class.

After a while, you learn to pace yourself. One of the greatest things I learned in college was how to say no. You learn your limits in college: what works for you, what doesn't. I know plenty of kids who can party all night and still function in class the next day. I was not that fortunate, but I learned to deal with it and came away with a degree.

Of course, college is totally what you make of it. Some students prefer to party away their four years; others schmooze with their professors for future letters of recommendation at their weekly office hour. I was somewhere in the middle, and I feel I experienced the full spectrum. I now have a bevy of crazy college stories as well as a periodic e-mail "Hey-how's-it-going?" relationship with one of my favorite professors. I came away with a sense of who I am, a new set of great friends, and great memories.

—*Tricia Powell*
Huntington Beach, California
University of California, Berkeley

COLLEGE AND COLLEGE STUDENTS are not what I imagined! At first, it seems intimidating because college is a new, big step in one's life. However, once you get to college, you'll see that this soon wears off and you become used to your surroundings and classes. You become motivated and this is what guides you through the next four years of your college life.

—*CARLY JACOBS*
PHILADELPHIA, PENNSYLVANIA
LA SALLE UNIVERSITY

WHEN YOU'RE IN HIGH SCHOOL, you picture college students as mature and sensible. When you get there, you realize they're probably less mature than high schoolers because these people are alone for the first time! Don't let your imagination run away with you. Many people preparing for college are going through the same anxiety as you are.

—*JOSH TIZEL*
TORONTO, ONTARIO
YORK UNIVERSITY

I pictured *Animal House* and wild parties. But we don't really have the Greek system at my school, so it's not even close!

—*MICHAEL NOBLE*
TORONTO, ONTARIO
YORK UNIVERSITY

KEEP THOSE GRADES UP

Colleges hope that you are continuing your academics strongly throughout your senior year. That means if you have been taking Honors and AP and IB classes, you should still take them. Be careful not to jeopardize your college admission at the end of the race. Senior grades can be critical to your admission; many colleges require them before they'll let you matriculate, and those that don't will call your high schools to obtain them if they are unsure about you. This happens regularly.

OTHER SIDE OF THE DESK: WATCH IT! WE CAN STILL SAY NO

Though it is often more of a threat than a reality, colleges can and do withdraw acceptances in cases of bad or illegal behavior. Colleges really do find out about everything, and you may be asked to write a letter about new and uncharacteristicly bad grades or a suspension, and explain what happened. Cheating and lying at schools with honor codes is especially serious—make sure you end on a high note your last semester; just do not risk your future.

I TRIED TO IMAGINE MYSELF FOUR YEARS in the future. I was trying to picture how my life would have changed in terms of things like, if I had a steady girlfriend or a car or a part- or full-time job. You have to realize that you will not be the same person coming out of college as going in. Your situation will be drastically different.

—*Sam Ulmer*
Newark, Delaware
University of Delaware

I ARRIVED AT COLLEGE AND REALIZED I was on my own and responsible for taking care of myself. I was far from my safety net (home), so it made me become more independent than ever. I really enjoyed the social aspect of it and had fun meeting new people from different backgrounds and cultures. I enjoyed some of my classes and joined a sorority, which was a great experience.

—*Anonymous*
New York, New York
Indiana University

MY HIGH SCHOOL VERSION of typical collegiate life: classes in the day, study at night, party on weekends; deep intellectual conversations on lawns in front of buildings; meeting friends and lovers who are just like you. The reality is nothing like that. Depending on the school, and your schedule, studying will be thrown in whenever you get a chance, partying either all the time or rarely (depending on the type of school you go to), and while you may find a person or two who share your passions, no one will ever be quite like you. And distrust all potential significant others: College is about the exploration of sex, not commitment. College will most definitely be great as long as you take chances, sign up for and try new things, but keep a smart head on your shoulders. Not all risks are to be taken.

—COURTNEY HEILMAN
BOSTON, MASSACHUSETTS

"MTV's version isn't exactly what college is about. Sure, there are fun spring-break parties, crazy dates, and adventures in college; but the studying certainly isn't glamorous. Studying wouldn't make for good television!"

—ANDREA
TORONTO, ONTARIO
QUEEN'S UNIVERSITY

SENIORITIS: A DISEASE, OR AN EXCUSE FOR FUN?

Once you get into college, all things associated with high school—such as tests, homework, and showing up on time (if at all)—shrink to microscopic importance. It's called senioritis, and it's real. But is it a good thing?

SENIORITIS: I HAD IT BAD. After I got into Stanford, it was so hard to concentrate on classes because I kept picturing sunny California with palm trees lining the streets. Luckily, teachers were sympathetic as the year ended. I normally wouldn't advocate playing hooky, but for graduating seniors already accepted to college, I'd say reward yourself by "being sick" a couple times so you get to sleep late. Once college hits, you'll wish you had slept more in high school.

—KATHERINE BELL
STANFORD, CALIFORNIA
STANFORD UNIVERSITY

• • • • • • • •

EMBRACE SENIORITIS: LEAVE SCHOOL EARLY FOR NO GOOD REASON. It's a nice feeling. You should have a pretty easy schedule. Load up on afternoon electives so you can go to the diner and then sleep.

—ZACHARY KLION
SUFFERN, NEW YORK
YALE UNIVERSITY

• • • • • • • •

TAKE CARE OF YOUR SCHOOLWORK FIRST. Don't worry about partying. If you work hard now, those partying days in college are going to be even better. It will be more worthwhile.

—ANDREW
DEARBORN, MICHIGAN
WAYNE STATE UNIVERSITY

TO BATTLE SENIORITIS, GIVE YOURSELF A GOAL. For example, graduating with a certain GPA. It will keep you in class and keep you focused, and in the end you'll do better.

—JENNIFER DRAGOVICH
SEMINOLE, FLORIDA
FLORIDA STATE UNIVERSITY

• • • • • • • •

SENIORITIS CAN BE A GOOD THING. Slacking off is a great way to spend time once colleges stop paying so much attention to high school academics.

—COLIN CAMPBELL
CHARLOTTESVILLE, VIRGINIA
UNIVERSITY OF NORTH CAROLINA

• • • • • • • •

I TRIED TO ENJOY THE LAST MOMENTS IN HIGH SCHOOL. When you get to college, you're on your own. Enjoy being taken care of. Be a kid.

—HANNAH ASSADI
SCOTTSDALE, ARIZONA
COLUMBIA COLLEGE

• • • • • • • •

DO NOT LET YOUR GRADES SLIP SENIOR YEAR! I totally slacked off and must have dropped three or four places in class rank. Not only did it cost me the opportunity to be in the top two of the class, but I was wait-listed at my first-choice college and I believe that my grades would eventually have caused me to be denied. I also think that the drop in grades cost me several scholarships.

—SHEILA CRAWFORD
RALEIGH, NORTH CAROLINA
NORTH CAROLINA STATE UNIVERSITY

THE WHOLE POINT OF SENIOR YEAR IS TO HAVE FUN. So, make sure you don't flunk out of school, but realize it's a year when you're the king. Revel in that, because in college you're kind of a small fish in a really, really big ocean.

—JENNI LERCHE
BELMONT, CALIFORNIA
BARNARD COLLEGE

JUST TAKE A DEEP BREATH and enjoy your last days of high school.

—DAVID
NEWARK, DELAWARE
VILLANOVA UNIVERSITY

SENIORITIS SET IN BEFORE I was even accepted to my college. It helped me to get out there and find out what I wanted to do.

—JULIE COLLINS
DES MOINES, IOWA
DRAKE UNIVERSITY

HEADS UP: TAKE ADVANTAGE!

To get off to a flying start academically and socially:

- Take advantage of orientation! This is a freebie period when you will never look stupid asking a lot of questions and bumbling around the campus. Everyone is a freshman in the same boat, so it is a safe period to explore and learn.
- Take advantage of all the school has to offer. The number one regret on everyone's list of what they missed in college? Not doing enough. Make sure you do attend at least a few of those great concerts, lectures, or football games so you never miss out. Getting involved in clubs adds great depth to your social life, too, so remember to force yourself to be brave and check things out.

GOING TO COLLEGE was a big step, because I am from Argentina. There, the education system is much different. You have to know what your career will be from a young age, and then you go to law school or medical school. So it was hard in the beginning with my family because they didn't understand anything about liberal arts degrees; there is no such thing in my country. But I loved this idea. I wanted to take a little bit of everything and educate myself in that way. In the end, my family wanted me to grow as a person. Now, they are supportive, but at the time it was hard.

—*HELIANA MEZZABOLTA*
BUENOS AIRES, ARGENTINA
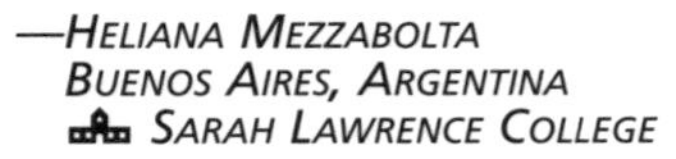
SARAH LAWRENCE COLLEGE

I HAD A PRETTY ROMANTICIZED NOTION of college: you know, sitting in the corner of a café and sipping lattes when I'm not in class, finding The One in one of my classes, and getting on the dean's list so I could go to graduate school. But once I got over the idea of college as a vacation from the immaturities of high school, it became a great place to be stimulated intellectually and socially. Four-year universities are not high schools. Prepare to be pushed, but most of all, prepare to push yourself. Try things that you didn't get to do in high school.

—*K.C.*
DAVIS, CALIFORNIA
UNIVERSITY OF CALIFORNIA, DAVIS

• • • • • • • •

FOR ME, COLLEGE WAS VERY MUCH like high school because I was living at home. I thought it would be more exciting, with lots of parties.

—*SHIRA*
TORONTO, ONTARIO
YORK UNIVERSITY

CLING TO CONTACTS

Good advice from admissions counselors: Keep up the relationship with the people you've come to know at your school. Even though you no longer "need" them, now that you've been admitted, those staff members and students you met during the application process may be the only people you'll know on campus (and who know you) at first. Say hi, drop them an e-mail, or share a coffee; never let a good connection wither.

COLLEGE IS AN ENTIRE INSTITUTION created for your development and performance. From the perspective of a current college student, these four years seem like a gift to play around with and learn as much about myself as I can. My experience has been one of facilitated introspection and discovery, with an emphasis on how to carry over my curiosity into my future.

—HEATHER MUNTZER
SANTA ROSA, CALIFORNIA
CALIFORNIA COLLEGE OF THE ARTS

"Have an open mind. It will be different. It will be tough. It will be the best experience of your life. You will be amazed by how much you grow as a person."

—ADRIENNE LANG
OLATHE, KANSAS
TEXAS CHRISTIAN UNIVERSITY

SOMETIMES YOU DON'T REALLY know who you are when you graduate high school, and going to college is really the opportunity to become who you want to be. I would hope that seniors wouldn't really stress themselves too much about how they're going to do in college. Just be yourself, and you'll find your right group of people. It will all fall into place.

—JULIE COLLINS
DES MOINES, IOWA
DRAKE UNIVERSITY

HOMEWORK MINUS THE HOME

You're going from a structured and restricted high school day of six to eight hours to a college school day of, typically, three hours. Sounds like paradise, but it can be a pitfall. How do you discipline yourself to study or stay engaged and focused? You have freedom, but it's an illusion. The work still needs to be done, but now it's all up to you.

Colleges are aware of the difficulty this transition poses for many students. Most schools provide an enormous amount of tutoring and academic support on campus. You don't have to qualify as a "special needs" student to need help: Go get it, at the first sign that you're falling behind.

COLLEGE IS SO MUCH BETTER! Nobody judges you. Everyone is an individual, and respected for it.

—Heidi
Yerington, Maine
Texas Southern University

• • • • • • • • •

COLLEGE IS WHAT I EXPECTED, because I tried not to expect anything!

—Briana
Sonoma, California
Sonoma State University

Last Summer Before College: Your To-Do List

Is the summer before college your farewell to freedom and youth? Your last moments at home, surrounded by the comforts (and annoyances) of family and old friends? One thing's certain: It's a unique time in your life that won't come again. You want to make sure you spend your time wisely. We asked other students what they did in their final summer before heading off to college. We also asked them what they would bring to college, if they could bring only one thing. Read on so that you can plan accordingly.

THE SUMMER BEFORE COLLEGE, I worked to save up money for school. If I did it over, I would've spent more time with friends and spent more time saying goodbye. Now, it's difficult for us to see one another.

—*JESSICA NEWMAN*
WEST BLOOMFIELD, MICHIGAN
MICHIGAN STATE UNIVERSITY

I DIDN'T DO ANYTHING TO PREPARE FOR COLLEGE BESIDES SHOP (WHICH WAS IMPORTANT, TOO!)

—*DANIELLA KANAL*
PITTSBURGH, PENNSYLVANIA
STERN COLLEGE

- Make a list of everything you think you'll need for school.
- Learn to create balance now between your work and your social life.
- Take advantage of your college's orientation program; it really does help.
- Begin now to broaden your world-view; explore new magazines or newspapers.
- Spend time with your friends and make plans to stay in touch.

COMING FOR ORIENTATION WAS EXTREMELY important because it helped me decide whether to live on campus, if I'd need a car, what's nearby, and just gave me an overall feel of things.

—*MAURA CALLAHAN*
TALLAHASSEE, FLORIDA
FLORIDA STATE UNIVERSITY

• • • • • • • • •

ACT LIKE YOU'RE NEVER GOING to see your friends again. Everyone always does, but it feels like you won't. Often, you grow apart from these people. Spend a lot of time with your family; you will miss them so much if you go far away.

—*ADRIENNE LANG*
OLATHE, KANSAS
TEXAS CHRISTIAN UNIVERSITY

I SPENT THE SUMMER BUYING EVERYTHING I thought I would need, attending orientation, trying to make as much money as possible, and enjoying my time with my friends and family.

—*Halli Levy*
Solon, Ohio
University of Missouri

THE SUMMER BEFORE COLLEGE I opted to travel. My goal was to expand my worldview as much as possible before college, as well as have a last hurrah with my high school friends. Some friends and I took a road trip around our state in the first part of the summer. In the month before I started college, I went to Finland and Estonia; it was an amazing experience that allowed me to try out my newly gained independence. I'm really glad I took the opportunity to go.

—*Amanda Nelson-Duac*
St. Augustine, Florida
George Washington University

Be sure not to worry too much about how things will work out. It all unfolds very smoothly.

—*David Danenberg*
Kent, Ohio
Kent State University

I WORKED AS A TEEN MENTOR and administrative assistant, and then traveled to Israel for a month. While I was there, I studied in a college for four weeks and got credits for school. I got in some traveling and still earned some credits along the way. I'm glad that I worked a bit and made some extra spending money for the rest of the year.

—*Elana Syrtash*
Toronto, Ontario
Stern College

HAVE FUN WITH FRIENDS that you know you won't be in touch with. This is what I did; we went sailing and to Cancun. It was a blast.

—*Rachann N. McKnight*
Houston, Texas
Indiana University

THE PREPARED PARENT

There are many ways a parent can help their children prepare for college:

- Make a checklist of all the things that need to be done, for example: doctor visits, get prescriptions filled, purchase dorm furnishings.

- Make a list of all the items that will be needed for school.

- Put together a survival kit of stamps, flashlight, addresses and phone numbers of important people such as physicians and family members.

- Let your child choose what he or she wants for the dorm from stores, then check off the list.

- A student shower would be a great idea to have for your child and help with the endless expense. Some stores even offer a student registry.

—*Phyllis Briskman Stanfield*
Pittsburgh, Pennsylvania
Washington and Jefferson College

THE SMARTEST THING WE DID to help our son make the transition to college was to sign him up for a pre-orientation program. He got into a small one—a rock and river outing—they spent several days whitewater rafting and rock climbing. He made five really good friends. These are the kids he eats dinner with now, and when we get his phone statement we can see these are the people he's communicating with. It really has helped him to have friends right away.

—Victoria Johnson
Minneapolis, Minnesota
P Skidmore College

I TOOK A CLASS AT MY COLLEGE, just to feel what it was like to not hear a bell ring when class is over. I took Introduction to Astronomy. It helped me understand how college works. There is really no more homework; it's studying and reading, so you have to have the willpower to actually do some work. It is a great feeling when you can go to class and understand what is being taught.

—Sarah Lola Palodichuk
Newport Beach, California

I WORKED THE SUMMER BEFORE my freshman year. I didn't really do anything school-wise. I had to read one book for a freshman reading project, and I had enough time to do that. A lot of kids like to take college-level courses over the summer and prepare before freshman year starts; but the most important thing is to balance academics with your social life. You don't want to go to school and start your university career without relaxing and taking a little break the summer before.

—Adam Kressel
Miami, Florida
Cornell University

Start packing early. It's not fun spending your last night at home surrounded by boxes and suitcases.

—Jessica
Saratoga, California
University of Southern California

GETTING READY FOR COLLEGE

As you are enjoying your last moments of youth, you're probably also wondering what you need to bring to college. We asked college students what they would choose if they could bring only one thing. Here are their "desert island" answers.

THE BEST PILLOW I COULD FIND. There is nothing like getting the rest you need ... especially when you have only three hours to get it in.

—*LINDSEY MORRISON GRANT*
PORTLAND, OREGON
CONCORDIA UNIVERSITY, PORTLAND

• • • • • • • •

A SCRAPBOOK. Make sure it has current pictures of friends and family you might be missing. Leave some room to add pictures of the new friends you will be making.

—*STEPHEN MACKAY*
SOUTH ORANGE, NEW JERSEY
UNIVERSITY OF CALIFORNIA, RIVERSIDE

• • • • • • • •

A PLANNER. It's hard to keep track of assignments, events, and activities without some serious organizational tools to help put things in perspective. I figured that out after the first term. Once I learned to budget my time, I noticed it became easier to focus. I set daily or weekly goals for myself and I didn't feel overwhelmed or like I needed to accomplish more than what was reasonable. As a result, I didn't burn out as quickly as other students.

—*SHANNON*
PORTLAND, OREGON
MARYLHURST UNIVERSITY

• • • • • • • •

PERSEVERANCE. College is easy until you stop showing up; then it becomes brutal and sometimes impossible. People who go to class pass that class. I've never seen someone fail who showed up. Never.

—*ADAM DREYFUS*
SAN FRANCISCO, CALIFORNIA
UNIVERSITY OF CONNECTICUT

I'D BRING MY BIKE. I used it to ride to classes after waking up late and being hung over from the night before. It really helped!

—MICHAEL ALBERT PAOLI
TORONTO, ONTARIO
UNIVERSITY OF TORONTO

• • • • • • • •

MY MOM: She would've done my laundry!

—BETH MAYEROWITZ
NEW YORK, NEW YORK
UNIVERSITY OF WISCONSIN

• • • • • • • •

I'D BRING LICORICE TO GIVE AWAY IN RESIDENCE: Candy will help you meet people and make friends!

—MICHAEL NOBLE
TORONTO, ONTARIO
YORK UNIVERSITY

• • • • • • • •

A FLAT-PANEL COMPUTER MONITOR; lugging a huge old one around while moving was not fun!

—K.C.
DAVIS, CALIFORNIA
UNIVERSITY OF CALIFORNIA, DAVIS

• • • • • • • •

A SLEEPING BAG, so that I could hang out at friends' places and have somewhere to sleep!

—SHIRA
TORONTO, ONTARIO
YORK UNIVERSITY

• • • • • • • •

AN OPEN AND CURIOUS MIND. College is a wonderful time to explore and learn about yourself.

—LISA GREENBAUM
NEW YORK, NEW YORK
RUTGERS UNIVERSITY

HERE IS WHAT I BROUGHT TO COLLEGE: a one-gallon tub of baking sprinkles, about 30 trucker hats, a shopping cart I converted into an armchair, all of my band T-shirts, my high school girlfriend, and all of the toiletries my mom hoped I would use. What of that *should* I have brought? The armchair.

—SETH
SUNNYVALE, CALIFORNIA
UNIVERSITY OF CALIFORNIA, BERKELEY

• • • • • • • •

MY LAPTOP. It's everything. When my laptop broke, it was a dark hour.

—MINEHAHA FORMAN
SAN ANTONIO VILLAGE, BELIZE
OAKLAND UNIVERSITY

• • • • • • • •

MY CAR. Once in a while you need to get away from the campus.

—JAMIE HARGRAVE
NUTLEY, NEW JERSEY
ROWAN UNIVERSITY

• • • • • • • •

ONE OF THOSE BIG ARMCHAIR-SHAPED PILLOWS. There are never any comfortable chairs in the dorm, so you put this thing on your bed against the wall, and voilà: instant armchair.

—NANCY POEHLMANN
ATLANTA, GEORGIA
AGNES SCOTT COLLEGE

• • • • • • • •

PICTURES AND SMALL MEMENTOS from high school and home.

—JESSICA PAULEY
CHILLICOTHE, OHIO
UNIVERSITY OF CINCINNATI

• • • • • • • •

PROBABLY MY LAPTOP. Actually, *definitely* my laptop.

—JESSICA
SARATOGA, CALIFORNIA
UNIVERSITY OF SOUTHERN CALIFORNIA

I WOULD BRING SOMETHING from someone whom you consider your best friend. I brought a box my sister made me with pictures and letters from everyone whom I could have ever hoped to write to me. A green box with maybe 20 envelopes inside would remind me of people who cared for me and who loved me unconditionally. Oh, and if you go to a place like Colgate, bring a heating blanket for your bed.

—JACKIE ADLAM
MILL VALLEY, CALIFORNIA
COLGATE UNIVERSITY

• • • • • • • •

FLEXIBILITY AND COURAGE. College uproots much of what you have known your entire childhood, and things you have never before confronted start to demand your attention.

—WHITNEY TRITT
ATLANTA, GEORGIA
WAKE FOREST UNIVERSITY

• • • • • • • •

BE SURE TO TAKE A PHOTO COLLAGE of friends and family to college with you. It's a good way not to get homesick. Also, it's good to share them with new friends so when you talk about those friends and family, you can include your new friends in your life.

—ANGELA MASSINI
CHICAGO, ILLINOIS
BUTLER UNIVERSITY

• • • • • • • •

SOMETHING THAT REMINDS you of your hometown. I am a big-time San Diego sports fan and always found it comforting to have posters and other items that represented where I was from.

—GARIN FAINSTEIN
SAN DIEGO, CALIFORNIA
UNIVERSITY OF SOUTHERN CALIFORNIA

• • • • • • • •

MY CHECKBOOK, preferably loaded! Life gets expensive.

—ADAM GUZOWSKI
SOUTH BEND, INDIANA
BALL STATE UNIVERSITY

I HAD SIX WEEKS OFF BETWEEN HIGH SCHOOL and summer session. I relaxed and baby-sat a lot. I wanted to earn money and do all the things that would be hard in college, like seeing my old friends. These days it's hard to see high school friends; when you come home on breaks, you want to see your family.

—LAUREN SHER
GAINESVILLE, FLORIDA
UNIVERSITY OF FLORIDA

Don't worry about saying goodbye to family and friends; you will talk to them often.

—MELISSA BERMAN
MANALAPAN, NEW JERSEY
MUHLENBERG COLLEGE

I WORKED THE SUMMER before school at the Silver Grill Café. It was a good idea because it gave me something to do and a way to save money. Ah, the Silver Grill!

—KYLE
FT. COLLINS, COLORADO
COLORADO STATE UNIVERSITY

I WAS SCARED TO LEAVE. I think everyone gets a little scared to leave home. I was scared because I was going to Illinois from Nebraska! I guess I just didn't want to realize that I was leaving home, so I procrastinated: I didn't start preparing to leave until a week or two before. I should have started getting ready sooner so I didn't feel so rushed. I could have enjoyed the last few weeks of my time at home.

—ANGELA FRIEDMAN
PEORIA, ILLINOIS
BRADLEY UNIVERSITY

COLLEGE IS AN ADJUSTMENT. There's suddenly a lack of parental control: do crazy things (like drink) the summer before so it won't mess up your studies later.

—BENN RAY
BALTIMORE, MARYLAND
SALISBURY UNIVERSITY

THE SUMMER BEFORE COLLEGE STARTED, I had AARO (Academic Advising, Registration, and Orientation) in which I spent two days with some fellow freshmen learning about the academics that SMU had to offer. I also did summer school at our local community college so that I could rack up some credits without having to spend an exorbitant amount of money. I took three courses that summer and got nine credit hours, which will help me graduate earlier.

—*JULIETA A. GRINFFIEL*
DALLAS, TEXAS
SOUTHERN METHODIST UNIVERSITY

START BUYING THINGS IN JUNE OR JULY so you can get your hands on everything you need. By August, the big stores will have less of what you want. Some stores have a registry online, and then the stuff is sent to your dorm so you don't have to overload your car.

—*MATT BORTNICK*
EAST BRUNSWICK, NEW JERSEY
INDIANA UNIVERSITY

I ENDED UP STARTING A COMPANY with a couple of friends and working all summer to make sure I had some extra cash. I recommend this; school costs more than you think it will.

—*P.T.*
ATLANTA, GEORGIA
PURDUE UNIVERSITY

I WENT TO AUSTRALIA for two weeks with my high school on an environmental trip. It was a great idea to do that before arriving on campus. It's good to get away and clear your head.

—*AMANDA NELSON*
NEW YORK, NEW YORK
UNIVERSITY OF WISCONSIN

TAKE ADVANTAGE OF ANY summer programs that your college offers to get a head start. Right before classes started, I entered a program with 40 other freshmen that allowed us to do some volunteer work and team-building activities in the community. It helped me feel like I made my college my home already, and I made new friends.

—Angela Massini
Chicago, Illinois
Butler University

• • • • • • • •

THE LAST SUMMER BEFORE COLLEGE, I traveled to Japan as the ambassador for my city's Sister City program. It was a wonderful learning experience that inspired me to spend the rest of my summer traveling to other places in Asia. If you can afford it, I would suggest traveling. And if you can do it with friends or family, all the better. The experience I had traveling to new places helped me be open to new things when I got to campus.

—Jocelyn Wang
Los Angeles, California
University of California, Los Angeles

• • • • • • • •

THERE WERE A LOT OF GOOD-BYES my last summer before college. Graduation was in May, but the good-bye period lasted all summer. See if you can organize one send-off event with all your friends. They all leave at staggered times, and it gets emotionally draining to say good-bye over and over. There are things that are sad to leave behind, so don't be afraid to mourn those. But there is a lot ahead for you to embrace!

—Whitney Tritt
Atlanta, Georgia
Wake Forest University

THE SUMMER BETWEEN HIGH SCHOOL and college is a great time to make some money for college: You'll sure need it when you get there. I found a summer job working at the zoo; it gave me some good experience with animals, as I would ultimately like to be a vet. Those are the kinds of experiences you can put on a résumé later to show that you were already thinking ahead.

—TED SASKIN
CAMPBELL, OHIO
KENT STATE UNIVERSITY

IF POSSIBLE, GO ON A SENIOR TRIP. I didn't, and I definitely wish that I had. It is kind of a rite of passage, going from a high school student to a college student. It symbolizes that transformation from childhood to adulthood, and from dependence to independence.

—JULIE ROBERTS
EDMOND, OKLAHOMA
UNIVERSITY OF OKLAHOMA

I REALLY JUST PARTIED MY WHOLE last summer away. I traveled around, and I was never home. I didn't have any goals. It was my last chance to have fun with friends at home. Don't just sit home and count the days or get nervous about missing home. Go to a friend's place for the weekend or to the shore for a week.

—MAREK DUDZIAK
BAYONNE, NEW JERSEY
LOYOLA COLLEGE

I RELAXED AND HUNG OUT WITH FRIENDS. I wanted to take it easy before entering a new time in my life; it helped with my adjustment.

—MAURA CALLAHAN
TALLAHASSEE, FLORIDA
FLORIDA STATE UNIVERSITY

Remember this: Freshman year is *tough*! It's a *huge* adjustment. Ultimately, be prepared to stick it out because it gets better.

—NICOLE SPENCE
WYCKOFF, NEW JERSEY
EMORY UNIVERSITY

I RELAXED EVERY DAY. Enjoy it. Don't burn bridges with people who aren't going to the same college as you—you'll be home at Thanksgiving, don't forget!

—*April*
Chicago, Illinois
Purdue University

YOUR LAST SUMMER BEFORE COLLEGE, live in that high school moment, but be ready to let go of it when September comes. You want to be as open as you can about meeting new friends and moving on.

—*Candace Watson*
Los Gatos, California
Santa Clara University

I THINK EXTRACURRICULAR ACTIVITIES are a good idea for more reasons than looking good on your college application. During high school, I volunteered for everything under the sun. I also took part in research projects and worked at the Center for Disease Control. All of this made me realize that there was more to life than academics. When I got to college, where I didn't need so many extra activities, I ended up doing them anyway, just for fun.

—*Janet*
Los Angeles, California
University of California, Los Angeles

More Wisdom: Good Stuff That Doesn't Fit Anywhere Else

Getting into college—and college itself—means challenging oneself with new experiences, learning from them, and moving on to new and better things. It means developing a personal perspective and living by it. That's about to happen to you. And as you get ready for the best four years of your life, here are some parting thoughts to help you along the way.

KEEP THIS IN MIND: Getting into college is not a test of your personal worth. When you apply to college, you're not applying to life. You're applying to an undergraduate program at an academic institution. The school has its own needs and wants that simply may not mesh with yours: Remember that.

—*BOBBY*
MAPLEWOOD, NEW JERSEY
UNIVERSITY OF CHICAGO

YOU WILL ONLY REGRET WHAT YOU *DON'T* DO.

—*ERIN PROTHRO*
REDWOOD CITY, CALIFORNIA
UNIVERSITY OF CALIFORNIA, LOS ANGELES

- Determine your own personal velocity—are you a dive-right-in or a toe-in-the-water person?
- College is the time to discover who you are and what you want to become.
- You may leave some old friends behind, but you'll also make some wonderful new ones.
- Find your passion, or be open-minded so it can find you.
- There is no one path to get to where you want to go.

DON'T GO CRAZY, but always follow your own path. An older friend of mine, who is consistently filled with good energy and advice, told me just last night, "Always forward, but never straight." That was the hardest part about preparing for college: staying on my own path. All of my friends were going to similar schools and I was crossing the state alone. I look back now and realize that going away to school without all of my best friends was one of my most fantastic decisions. I graduated and moved west. Most of them are still back in my hometown and have not experienced half the life that I have lived.

—HILLARY
BRECKENRIDGE, COLORADO
BOWLING GREEN STATE UNIVERSITY

WHERE YOU GO TO COLLEGE is nowhere near as important as they make it out to be. College is more a personal growing experience than anything else. While degree A may net you X amount of money upon hiring, as opposed to degree B netting you Y amount, college and post-college is really about making it on your own. If you make the effort, you should have an amazing experience in the long run.

—*DAVID BERNGARTT*
CHAPEL HILL, NORTH CAROLINA
UNIVERSITY OF NORTH CAROLINA

"Advice to parents: It's more important that your child is happy than that you display a 'Harvard' window decal on your SUV. Deep down, you already know this."

—*ANONYMOUS*
NEW YORK, NEW YORK
BELOIT COLLEGE

WHEN I FIRST STARTED LOOKING into schools in the United States, I didn't speak any English. Instead of applying to schools I wanted to attend, I decided to do a one-year intensive English as a Second Language program at a community college. Doing that was incredible. I learned quickly, and this opened many doors for me.

—*ANONYMOUS*
ARGENTINA
SARAH LAWRENCE COLLEGE

I LEARNED THE HARD WAY that your best friend is not necessarily going with you to college. My friend Beth and I had planned on going through the whole thing together. But toward the end it was obvious her grades were not going to get her into the schools I was considering. It was devastating to both of us. I learned that you need to make your college choice individually. You will become a better person if you are brave enough to strike out on your own.

—Colleen Bakey
Frederick, Maryland
Georgetown University

• • • • • • • •

I THINK MORE PEOPLE NEED TO GET OUT and spend time in a different region of the country; it's an education that goes beyond the classroom. For me, I left my family and friends behind and didn't know anyone within a 500-mile radius of my campus. I wanted to experience a new place and meet new people; I wouldn't trade my time here for anything.

—Scott Coolbaugh
Knoxville, Tennessee
University of Tennessee

• • • • • • • •

ONE THING I WISH I had discovered earlier: College Parents of America (www.collegeparents.org). It is a national membership organization that provides access to test-prep courses like Kaplan and Thomson Peterson's as well as, scholarship searches through FindTuition.com. They maintain a parents resource center and distribute a quarterly e-newsletter for parents, customized to a student's high school graduation year.

—Nancy Nelson-Duac
Granbury, Texas
George Washington University

I DECIDED EARLY ON THAT I wanted to go to Youngstown State, not because it's close to home but because it has a great mathematics department. I knew my grades in high school weren't going to blow anybody away, so I knew it might take me a little while to get in. There were other schools that would have taken me right after high school, but I wanted to go to YSU. So I went to community college for two semesters and applied again. This time they accepted me. Pick the school that is right for you and then don't take no for an answer. Even if it takes a little longer to get in, you'll have your whole life to reap the rewards of your patience.

—Dan Montoya
Youngstown, Ohio
Ohio State University

COLLEGE IS IN SOME WAYS easier than high school because the classes are spread out. As a Smittcamp Scholar, I had to take more challenging classes than other students, but when I'm challenged I do better work. On the other hand, it took a while to get used to staying in classes for longer periods. The best thing to do is take notes and meet people in the class whom you can study with or talk to about the class. College is the best time to discover what drives you, what bores you, and what you may want to do with your future. Students need to dig deep down and listen to what their spirit tells them. Do what you enjoy doing. Choose a path that inspires you, so that you don't feel trapped by your decision. Getting a degree and going to college should be a wonderful experience if you allow yourself to apply yourself to something you enjoy.

—Emily Tuck
Fresno, California
California State University

Don't decide what you want to do with your life when you're 18. You don't know yet. Just get into college and get a couple of years out of the way. Then decide.

—Kira
St. Petersburg, Florida
SPC/PTA Program

PARENT TO PARENT

TELL YOUR KIDS THAT YOU LOVE THEM, TRUST THEM, and are proud of them when they are going through applying to schools. Trust that all the great parenting you've done in the past (and even the not-so-great moments) has provided a guide and foundation for your child to make good decisions.

—*BRIANA*
SONOMA, CALIFORNIA
P SONOMA STATE UNIVERSITY

A FRIEND OF MINE WHOSE CHILD IS ALREADY IN COLLEGE TOLD ME that at the end of the day it's your child's future, not yours. In other words, you have to know when to back off. The final say cannot be yours because the rewards or failures will not be yours to enjoy or suffer through.

—*COLTON CHAMPNEY*
BALTIMORE, MARYLAND
P UNIVERSITY OF MARYLAND

I WISH WE HAD KNOWN THAT taking on too many credits at the beginning and trying to fulfill graduation requirements in your first semester is not a smart idea. The transition into college is a very big step involving educational aspects of school, as well as the entire new experience of living on your own. Taking on too much at the beginning can cause all the parts of the college experience to suffer. It is much better to start out a little slower and build self-confidence, then move on to the harder courses once the student understands the college process.

—*J.K.D.*
PITTSBURGH, PENNSYLVANIA
P KENT STATE UNIVERSITY

The process clouds the minds of parents. Maybe of kids, too.

—*ANONYMOUS*
BROOKLYN, NEW YORK
P BARD COLLEGE

GOING AWAY FROM HOME is a good idea and a good experience, if you or your parents can afford it. My mom really wanted her kids to go away because she felt like it was the best thing she did. Now that I've done that, I agree with her advice.

—*JANNA HAROWITZ*
VANCOUVER, BRITISH COLUMBIA
MCGILL UNIVERSITY

I TRULY BELIEVE YOU CAN GET a great education and a great launch into adult life at hundreds of colleges, if you are ready for it and open to it. And that's a matter of maturity, which kids have in varying amounts. We have really bought into the consumer marketing junk of colleges, where going to Yale is like buying a BMW. We also believe in the idea of an American meritocracy, when really, it does not exist.

—*ANONYMOUS*
NEW YORK, NEW YORK
CARLETON COLLEGE

I'M A BIG FAN OF THE BRITISH method of the gap year. When you finish the equivalent of high school, you take off six months to a year and travel and work abroad. I think that's a great thing to do. Give yourself some time to wander around and think about what you want and who you want to be. It's very important for people at that age. There's school, and then there's the school of life.

—Jessamyn Goshom
Washington, D.C.
University of Maryland, College Park

• • • • • • • •

STUDY WHAT YOU ARE PASSIONATE ABOUT, but be smart. At the least, minor in something that will get you a job, be it computer science, business, accounting, or teaching. Speaking as a recent honors grad with a B.A. in English and a 3.79 GPA, no employer cares how smart you are if you aren't proficient with computers and have some marketable skills. Also, what you may think you want to do when you're applying may change when you get into your classes.

—Erin
Tacoma, Washington

• • • • • • • •

THOUGH AT THE TIME IT SEEMS like the college admissions process is the most important thing in the world, it's not. Don't lose sight of the bigger, more important things, like developing relationships with your friends and enjoying the memories of your senior year. Be careful not to lose friends over the competition; be happy for one another regardless of the circumstances, because after you graduate, the college admissions process is a trivial detail of the distant past.

—Elana Brownstein
Baltimore, Maryland
University of Maryland, College Park

Really useful web sites

Check these sites for whatever information you may need. In addition, the Web sites of each college or university you are interested in will provide specific information.

FUNDING

Ameri-Corps National & Community Service
www.cns.gov

Gates Millennium Scholars
www.gmsp.org

FAFSA Express
www.fafsa.ed.gov

FastWEB
www.fastweb.com

The Financial Aid Information Page
www.finaid.org

Free Scholarship Search
www.freschinfo.com

MOLIS Scholarship Service
Content.sciencewise.com/newscholarship/scholarships3.cfm

Sallie Mae CASHE Scholarship Service
Scholarships.salliemae.com
www.wiredscholar.com

Scholarship Search
Cbweb10p.collegeboard.org/fundfinder/html/fundfind01.html

Student Advantage
Scholaraid.studentadvantage.com

The Student Guide
http://studentaid.ed.gov

Higher Education Services Organization
www.hesc.com

NCAA Guide for the College Bound Student Athlete
www.ncaa.org

New York's College Savings Program
www.nysaves.org

Unusual Scholarships
http://finaid.org/scholarships/unusual.phtml

David Lynch Foundation for Consciousness-Based Educations and World Peace
www.davidlynchfoundation.org

Expected Family Contributions Calculator
https://apps.collegeboard.com/fincalc/servlet/efcCalulatorServlet

Financial Aid Calculators
www.finaid.org/calculatrors/finaidestimate.phtml
estudentloan.com

Scholarship Searches
www.collegenet.com
www.scholarship.com

Qualified Minority Scholarship Search
http://www.molis.org/

Hispanic Online
www.hispaniconline.com/edu&

Coalition of Asian Pacific American Youth
www.capayus.org

Jackie Robinson Foundation
www.jackierobinson.org

United Negro College Fund
www.uncf.org

ASPIRA
www.aspira.org

American Indian Movement
www.aimovement.org

ORIENTATION

GEAR UP
www.ed.gov/gearup/index.html

Campus Tours
www.campustours.com

The U
www.theU.com

College Bound Interactive Guide to Student Life
www.cbnet.com

FINDING YOUR SCHOOL

The College Board
www.collegeboard.com

Commission on Independent Colleges and Universities
www.nycolleges.org

Peterson's Education Center
www.petersons.com

Project EASI (Easy Access for Students and Institutions)
http://easi.ed.gov

College Search
www.citizensbank.com/edu

RESOURCES FOR SCHOOLS AND FAMILIES

Universal Black Pages
www.ubp.com

US News & World Report
www.usnews.com/usnews/edu/grad/rankings/rankindex.htm

American Universities
www.clas.ufl.edu/CLAS/american-universities.html

College Opportunities Online
nces.ed.gov/IPEDS/cool/COOLHome.asp

American Association of Community Colleges
www.aacc.nche.edu

Community College Web
www.mcli.dist.maricopa.edu/cc

Database of Colleges
www.collegenet.com
www.gocollege.com

College Search Sites
www.collegeedge.com

Campus Dirt
www.campusdirt.com/

College Confidential
www.Collegeconfidential.com

College Prowler
CollegeProwler.com

TESTING & APPLYING

The American College Testing Program
www.act.org

Educational Testing Services
www.ets.org

TEST.com
www.test.com

Princeton review
www.review.com

Sylvan Leaning Centers
www.educate.com

The Common Application
www.commonapp.org

AAPZAP
www.collegeview.com/aapzap

Kaplan On-Line
www.kaplan.com

GRE
www.gre.org

PRAXIS
www.teachingandlearning.org

SAT
www.collegeboard.org/sat

TOEFL
Web1.toefl.org

College Link
www.collegelink.com

College Net
www.collegenet.com

Thick Envelope
www.Thickenvelope.com

National League for Nursing
www.nin.org/test

COUNSELING

National Association for College Admission Counseling
www.nacac.org

College Horizons
www.whitneylaughlin.com

Internet Guide for Parents
www.GuideforParents.com

GAP YEAR PROGRAMS

www.gap-year.com
www.yearoutgroup.org
www.leapnow.org/home.htm
www.bunac.org
www.interimprograms.com/sampleprograms/index.asp
www.transitionsabroad.com/listings/work/shortterm/gap_year_jobs_abroad.shtml
www.traveltree.co.uk/pages/gap-year-programs.asp

MISCELLANEOUS

College is Possible
www.collegeispossible.org

Trio Programs
www.trioprograms.org

Yes I Can
www.yesican.gov

The Chronicle of Higher Education
http://chronicle.com

CREDITS

Page 3: *The Early College High School Initiative*
Page 18: "Ivy League colleges find 2006 is a buyer's market," MSN, April 14, 2006.
Page 23: "Can't Complete High School? Go Right to College," Karen W. Arenson, *New York Times*, May 30, 2006.
Page 33: "Taming the Monster," *New York Times*, April 23, 2006.
Page 36: "Chewing gum selectively improves memory in healthy volunteers." Wilkinson L., Scholey A., Wesness K., *Appetite*. June 2002
Page 39: *American Educator*, Spring 2004.
Page 46: "The Long (and Sometimes Expensive) Road to the SAT," Julie Bick, *New York Times*, May 28, 2006.
Page 48: Betsy F. Woolf, Admit U College and Graduate School Admissions Consulting, Westchester, NY.
Page 49: "Taming the Monster," *New York Times*, April 23, 2006.
Page 51: Betsy F. Woolf, Admit U College and Graduate School Admissions Consulting, Westchester, NY.
Page 59: "Ivy League colleges find 2006 is a buyer's market," MSN, April 14, 2006.
Page 62: Betsy F. Woolf, Admit U College and Graduate School Admissions Consulting, Westchester, NY.
Page 65: "In New Twist on College Search, a First Choice, and 20 Backups," *New York Times*, March 21, 2006.
Page 75: The Cooperative Institutional Research Program at U.C.L.A. as reported in the *New York Times*, March 21, 2006.
Page 81: Kerry Keegan, College Admissions Counselor, Academy of the Holy Names, Tampa, FL; *New York Times*, March 21, 2006; Betsy F. Woolf, Admit U College and Graduate School Admissions Consulting, Westchester, NY.
Page 98: "Student resume padding result of college selection process," *The Orlando Sentinel*, March 16, 2006.
Page 100: *The Princeton Review*, www.princetonreview.com/college/research/articles/prepare/summerbook3.asp
Page 122: Questions for Your Visit, *College View*, www.collegeview.com/articles/CV/application/questions_for_visit.html
Page 131: "America's Best Colleges 2006," *U.S. News & World Report*.
Page 135: *The Scholarship Book 2003*. Prentice Hall Press: New Jersey, 2002. p.vii.
Page 139: Education Life, *New York Times*, January 2006.
Page 145: Education Life, *New York Times*, January 2006.
Page 160: "Private counselors help students reach goals," *The Pittsburgh Tribune-Review*, September 27, 2005.

Page 172: Betsy F. Woolf, Admit U College and Graduate School Admissions Consulting, Westchester, NY.

Page 175: Kerry Keegan, College Admissions Counselor, Academy of the Holy Names, Tampa, FL.

Page 185: "Ivy League colleges find 2006 is a buyer's market," MSN, April 14, 2006.

Page 189: "When a Risqué Online Persona Undermines a Chance for a Job," Alan Finder, *New York Times*, June 11, 2006.

Page 190: Betsy F. Woolf, Admit U College and Graduate School Admissions Consulting, Westchester, NY; Kerry Keegan, College Admissions Counselor, Academy of the Holy Names, Tampa, FL.

Page 193: Kerry Keegan, College Admissions Counselor, Academy of the Holy Names, Tampa, FL; Betsy F. Woolf, Admit U College and Graduate School Admissions Consulting, Westchester, NY.

Page 204: "Group names top 10 conservative colleges," *WorldNetDaily*, December 16, 2005.

Page 211: www.campusdirt.com.

Page 213: "The Electronic Lowdown on Colleges," Michelle Slatalla, New York Times, March 9, 2006; Education Life, *New York Times*, January 2006.

Page 214: Education Life, *New York Times*, January 2006.

Page 228: Kerry Keegan, College Admissions Counselor, Academy of the Holy Names, Tampa, FL.

Page 230: Kerry Keegan, College Admissions Counselor, Academy of the Holy Names, Tampa, FL.

SPECIAL THANKS

Thanks to our intrepid "headhunters" for going out to find so many respondents from around the country with interesting advice to share:

Jamie Allen, Chief Headhunter

Alexa Stanard
Andrea Fine
Andrea Syrtash
Ashley Spicer
Beshaleba Rodell
Carly Milne
Elana Brownstein
Gloria Averbuch
Helen Bond
Janet Frishberg
Jennifer Bright Reich
Ken McCarthy
Linda Lincoln
Liz Garone
Marie Suszynski
Sally Burns
Stacey Shannon
Staci Siegel

Thanks, too, to our editorial advisor Anne Kostick. And thanks to our assistant, Miri Greidi, for her yeoman's work at keeping us all organized. The real credit for this book, of course, goes to all the people whose experiences and collective wisdom make up this guide. There are too many of you to thank individually, of course, but you know who you are.

ADVICE FROM:

Agnes Scott College
American University
Anderson University
Austin Community College
Ball State University
Bard College
Barnard College
Beloit College
Boston University
Bowling Green State University
Bradley University
Brandeis University
Brooks Institute of Photography
Brown University
Butler University
California College of the Arts
California State University
Carleton College
Central Michigan University
Chatham College
Colgate University
Colorado State University
Columbia College
Columbia University
Concordia University, Portland
Coppin State University
Cornell University
Drake University
East Christian College
Eckerd College
Emory University
Florida State University
George Mason University
George Washington University
Georgetown University
Grand Valley State University
Harvard University
Indiana University
Kent State University
Knox College
La Salle University
Lafayette College
Louisiana State University
Loyola College
Marquette University
Marylhurst University
McGill University
Michigan State University
Mount Holyoke College
Muhlenberg College
New York University
North Carolina State University
North Dakota State University
North Iowa Area Community College
Oakland University
Ohio State University
Ohio University
Oklahoma Baptist University
Point Loma Nazarene University
Princeton University
Purdue University
Queen's University
Richland College, Dallas County Community College District
Rowan University
Rutgers University
Salisbury University
Santa Clara University
Sarah Lawrence College
Seton Hall University
Seton Hill University
Skidmore College
Sonoma State University
Southern Methodist University
Southwestern University
Stanford University
State University of New York, Purchase College
State University of New York, University at Buffalo
State University of New York, College at Brockport
Stern College for Women
Syracuse University
Texas Christian University
Texas Southern University
Texas State University
Tulane University
University of Arizona
University of Baltimore
University of California
University of Chicago
University of Cincinnati
University of Colorado
University of Connecticut
University of Delaware
University of Florida
University of Illinois
University of Kansas
University of Maryland, College Park
University of Michigan
University of Missouri
University of North Carolina
University of Oklahoma
University of Pennsylvania
University of Southern California
University of Tennessee
University of Toronto
University of Virginia
University of Wisconsin
Vanderbilt University
Villanova University
Wake Forest University
Washington and Jefferson College
Wayne State University
West Virginia University
Western Illinois University
Yale University
York University
Youngstown State University

TELL US YOUR STORY™

... and join Hundreds of Heads®.

Become one of the hundreds of smart and funny voices of experience whose collected wisdom makes our books so great. Survived a life experience and learned a lesson from it? Keep a mental list of do's and don'ts? Know an amazing story that happened to a friend or relative? Tell us about it. Share your advice, get published, and join the hundreds of contributors to the series.

Click on **www.hundredsofheads.com** to:

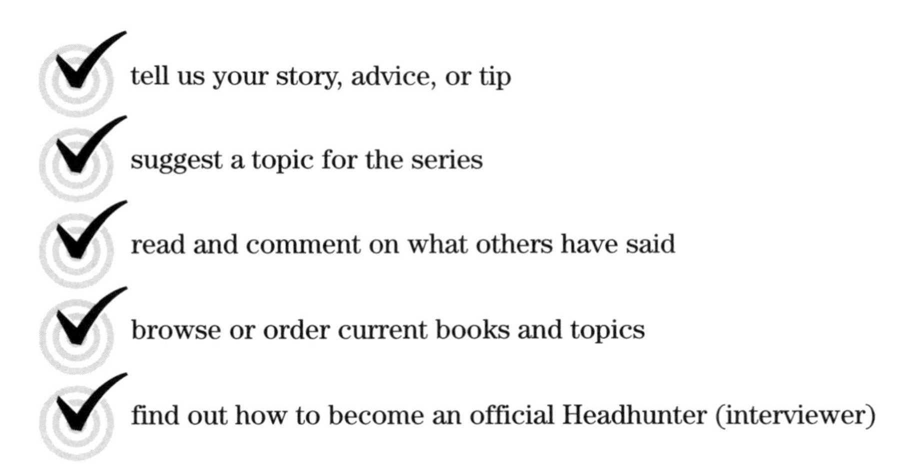

- tell us your story, advice, or tip
- suggest a topic for the series
- read and comment on what others have said
- browse or order current books and topics
- find out how to become an official Headhunter (interviewer)

www.hundredsofheads.com

CHECK OUT OTHER BOOKS FROM HUNDREDS OF HEADS®

HOW TO SURVIVE DATING...by Hundreds of Happy Singles Who Did (and some things to avoid, from a few broken hearts who didn't) (248 pages, $12.95)

ISBN-10: 0-9746292-1-9
ISBN-13: 978-0974-62921-6

"Whether you are single or not, *How to Survive Dating* will have you rolling with laughter .... The book contains hundreds of pearls of wisdom .... This isn't your ordinary dating book."

—TRUE ROMANCE

Rated one of the top 10 Dating Books

—*ABOUT.COM*

"Invaluable advice .... If I had read this book before I made my movie, it would have been only *10 Dates*."

—*MYLES BERKOWITZ, FILMMAKER*
WROTE, DIRECTED, AND WENT OUT ON 20 DATES *FOR FOX SEARCHLIGHT*

"It's like having a few hundred friends on speed-dial."

---*KNIGHT RIDDER/TRIBUNE NEWS SERVICE*

HOW TO LOSE 9,000 LBS. (OR LESS): Advice from 516 Dieters Who Did (240 pages, $13.95)

ISBN-10: 0-9746292-8-6
ISBN-13: 978-09746292-8-5

As seen in *Women's World* magazine

"Keep motivated with a little help from real folks when you turn to the new book *How to Lose 9,000 Lbs. (or Less)* ... the book offers oodles of down-to-earth tips and solutions in short snippets from more than 500 dieters."

—DALLAS NEWS

"Ingenious, often hilarious, advice from real people ... "

—COURIER POST, *NEW JERSEY*

"Great advice on motivation, choosing a diet, avoiding temptation, healthy eating, exercise, medical help (from pills to surgery), keeping the weight off, and more."

—*KNIGHT RIDDER/TRIBUNE*

“This how-to book is jam-packed with hundreds of quick tips and great advice … ”

—San Diego Family Magazine

“Words of wisdom: Hundreds of parents nationwide weigh in with advice on everything from messy bedrooms to driving to sex … ”

—The Cincinnati Enquirer

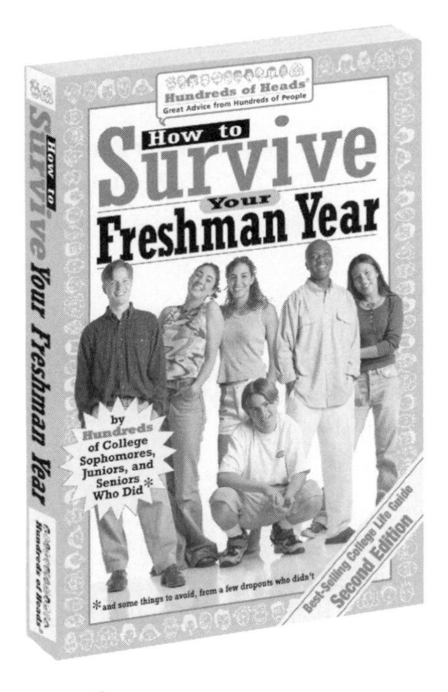

 #1 bestselling college life guide in an updated second edition

 Over 1,000 pieces of advice from students at more than 100 colleges

 All-new tips, facts, references, and checklists for college-bound teens

 Short, entertaining stories make a fun and quick read

 The perfect high school graduation gift!

HOW TO SURVIVE YOUR TEENAGER …by Hundreds of Still-Sane Parents Who Did (and some things to avoid, from a few whose kids drove them nuts) (256 pages, $13.95)

ISBN-10: 0-9746292-3-5
ISBN-13: 978-0974-62923-0

HOW TO SURVIVE YOUR FRESHMAN YEAR…by Hundreds of Sophomores, Juniors, and Seniors Who Did (and some things to avoid, from a few dropouts who didn’t) SECOND EDITION (256 pages, $13.95)

ISBN-10: 1-933512-04-0
ISBN-13: 978-1933512-04-4

WHAT THE CRITICS ARE SAYING ABOUT *HOW TO SURVIVE YOUR FRESHMAN YEAR*

Book of the Year Award finalist, *Foreword* magazine

Recommended Reading, *Positive Teens* magazine

Ingram Library Service "Hidden Gem"

Included in "Ten Good Books for Grads," *Detroit Free Press*

"A guide full of fantastic advice from hundreds of young scholars who've been there .... a quick and fun read."

—Boston Herald, *Teen News*

"The perfect send-off present for the student who is college bound. The book manages to be hilarious and helpful. As an added bonus, it's refreshingly free of sanctimony."

—The Post and Courier, *Charleston, South Carolina*

"This book proves that all of us are smarter than one of us."

—*John Katzman, Founder and CEO, Princeton Review*

"Honest portrait of the trials and jubilations of college and how to best navigate your own way through."

—Next Step *Magazine*

"Explains college to the clueless."

—College Bound Teen

"The advice dispensed is handy, useful, and practical. This book will make great light reading for an incoming freshman."

—Voya

"A great tool for young people beginning an important and often daunting new challenge, with short and funny, real-world tips."

—Washington Parent

Visit www.hundredsofheads.com to learn more.

WHAT THE CRITICS ARE SAYING ABOUT HUNDREDS OF HEADS®:

"The next 'Dummies' or 'Chicken Soup' … offers funny but blunt advice from thousands across America who've walked some of life's rougher roads."

—DEMOCRAT AND CHRONICLE *(ROCHESTER, NEW YORK)*

"Colorful bits of advice…So simple, so entertaining, so should have been my million-dollar idea."

—THE COURIER-JOURNAL *(LOUISVILLE, KENTUCKY)*

"The books have struck a nerve. 'Freshman Year' was the number-one-selling college life guide of 2004 … "

—*CNN.COM*

"The series … could be described as 'Chicken Soup for the Soul' meets 'Worst Case Scenario.'"

—*ATLANTA BUSINESS CHRONICLE*

"Move over, 'Dummies' … Can that 'Chicken Soup!' Hundreds of Heads are on the march to your local bookstore!"

—*ELIZABETH HOPKINS, KFNX (PHOENIX, ARIZONA) RADIO HOST,* THINKING OUTSIDE THE BOX

"Hundreds of Heads hopes to make life in our complicated new millennium a bit more manageable."

—THE RECORD *(HACKENSACK, NEW JERSEY)*

ABOUT THE EDITOR

RACHEL KORN is a U.S. college advisor and consultant. She attended Brandeis University as a Justice Brandeis Scholar, and Harvard University, where she earned a Master's Degree in Higher Education Administration. Rachel worked on the admissions staffs at Wellesley College, Brandeis University, and The University of Pennsylvania, where she visited hundreds of high schools across the nation, interviewed prospective students, and read and advised committees on approximately 10,000 applications. She has been an active member of several professional organizations including regional chapters of the National Association for College Admissions Counseling and the College Board. Rachel currently lives in Tel Aviv, Israel.